"Whether you're having a quarterlife crisis, or if you just want an insider's guide to the working world, read this book. It will teach you how to get your career on track by developing a personal mission statement, accentuating the positive, and making well-informed decisions. Sage advice from a gifted young writer."

—Ken Blanchard, Coauthor of *The One Minute Manager®* and *The Leadership Pill*

"There's only one thing I hate about this book: that I didn't have it when I was in my 20s! In a compelling and eminently readable volume, Levit lays out the secrets that it takes most of us at least a decade—and a lot of mistakes—to discover."

—Rachel Solar-Tuttle, Coauthor of *Table Talk: The Savvy Girl's Alternative to Networking*

"This book explodes with practical and relevant advice for young professionals who want to master the fast track *yesterday.* As an insider who has battled Corporate America and won, Levit offers a no-nonsense approach that gets to the heart of what really works."

—Harry E. Chambers, Author of *Getting Promoted: Real Strategies for Advancing Your Career*

"After four years of jeans and baseball caps, and three hours of class a day, workforce newbies need a boot camp like this to face up to the rigors of the working week."

—Abby Wilner, Coauthor of *Quarterlife Crisis: The Unique Challenges of Life in Your Twenties*

"Alexandra Levit has written a savvy, informative guide for first-timers making their way in the corporate world. Reading this book will get college grads moving in the right direction."

—Stacy Kravetz, Author of *Welcome to the Real World: You've Got an Education—Now Get a Life!*

They Don't Teach Corporate in College

A Twenty-Something's Guide
to the Business World

Alexandra Levit

CAREER
PRESS

Franklin Lakes, NJ

THEY DON'T TEACH CORPORATE IN COLLEGE
EDITED BY GINA M. CHESELKA
TYPESET BY STACEY A. FARKAS
Cover design by DesignConcept
Printed in the U.S.A. by Book-mart Press

To order this title, please call toll-free 1-800-CAREER-1 (NJ and Canada: 201-848-0310) to order using VISA or MasterCard, or for further information on books from Career Press.

CAREER
PRESS

The Career Press, Inc., 3 Tice Road, PO Box 687,
Franklin Lakes, NJ 07417
www.careerpress.com

Library of Congress Cataloging-in-Publication Data
Levit, Alexandra, 1976-
   They don't teach corporate in college : a twenty-something's guide to the business world / by Alexandra Levit.
      p. cm.
   Includes bibliographical references and index.
   ISBN 1-56414-765-7 (paper)
   1. Business--Vocational guidance. 2. Success in business. I. Title.

HF5381.L48 2004
650.1'084'2—dc22

                                                    2004051967

Dedication

For my husband and partner in life

—Stewart Shankman—

who reads every word.

Acknowledgements

This book is the result of years of personal experience in the workplace, as well as valuable input from the following talented individuals: Ken Blanchard, Harry Chambers, Judith Gerberg, David Gordon, Stacy Kravetz, Linda Price, Karen Schaffer, Mark Schwartz, Rachel Solar-Tuttle, Neil Stroul, Bruce Tulgan, and Abby Wilner.

A round of applause goes out to those who helped turn a good idea into a published book: my incredibly supportive agent at Trident Media Group, Alex Glass; my generous friend Peter Castro (who introduced me to Alex); my patient and wise lawyer, Josh Grossman; my editor, Gina M. Cheselka; and the rest of the very competent and always responsive staff at The Career Press—Ron Fry, Stacey Farkas, Clayton W. Leadbetter, Michael Lewis, Kirsten Beucler, Linda Rienecker, and Michael Pye.

I will be forever grateful to the dozens of corporate twenty-somethings who inspired me with their personal stories.

Finally, I'd like to thank my friends, my colleagues through the years, and my family—especially my parents, Robert and Ferne Levit, for keeping the faith and encouraging me each step of the way.

Contents

Introduction

After I graduated from college, I was hell-bent on moving to New York City. I believed in the saying, "If you can make it in New York, you can make it anywhere." I was the type of kid who studied hard and got As in school, and I didn't think I'd have any trouble skipping up the corporate ladder in one of the most intimidating cities in the world. When I landed a job in a top public relations firm despite zero relevant experience, I thought the toughest part was over. I dumped my extra resumes in a recycling bin and eagerly awaited a paycheck that would scarcely cover my rent. I looked forward to worldly business trips, stimulating office brainstorms, and hanging out with my coworkers every Friday at happy hour.

Three years later, I found myself cringing at the words *corporate travel*, and I had never made it to a happy hour gathering because I was passed out on the couch every Friday night. One of my managers disliked me so much that I was convinced I had killed her in a past life. I held an entry-level position for 16 months while people with half my intelligence and work ethic lapped me. I saw a career counselor, book-marked Monster.com on my browser, and dreamt of a distant future in which I was happily ensconced in a job that merited getting up in the morning. My resume listed four positions in three years because I was always on the lookout for a better opportunity that would bring the ever-elusive job satisfaction I dreamt of.

Desperate for help, I looked in Barnes & Noble for a book geared toward twenty-somethings struggling to survive in the corporate world. I found a handful of titles on finding an affordable living situation, decoding tax forms, and allocating the right combination to one's brand spanking new 401(k) plan. And I assure you, after painting these books with a yellow highlighter, I had the best damn 401(k) in the world. My 401(k) was so sound that I could have been a billionaire by the time I retired from my chief general manager, divisional senior vice president position at age 65!

Too bad I wouldn't last that long. The way I was going, I would be the corporate equivalent of the dinosaur in Darwin's natural selection process. In those days, I spent a lot of time in bars doing tequila shots and smoking cigarettes. I complained to anyone who would listen about the death of common sense in the workplace, and how my expensive undergraduate education was being wasted on clearing paper jams from the Xerox machines. When I probed my mother for answers, she told me that life wasn't supposed to be fair or fulfilling, and that I should learn to tolerate my job. My father shrugged and said he hoped I would become the first in a long line of suffering, worker-bee Levits to triumph in the business world...but he doubted it. My friends told me to go to law school.

The idea of going back to school was tempting indeed, and why not? We're comfortable with the concept of school. We know how the story goes: If you work hard, you get good grades and everyone is happy. The business world, however, is another animal entirely. Politically motivated and fraught with nonsensical change, the corporate world is not a natural fit for graduates who leave school expecting results from a logical combination of education and effort. Suddenly, the tenets of success we were taught since kindergarten don't apply, because getting ahead in the business world has nothing to do with intelligence or exceeding a set of defined expectations. In our first corporate jobs, we come up against rules no one ever told us about. We feel lost. It's like we were whisked away on a spaceship and have landed on an alien planet where we have to eat oxygen and breathe vegetables.

So how did I survive it? Well, things started to turn around when I finally realized that the corporate world is the same everywhere—and I was the same person I always was. I was bringing my misguided attitudes and beliefs about the business world to each new position, and I knew I wouldn't be successful until I changed them. So I stopped job jumping and started taking courses and reading books on practical self-improvement. I put myself under a microscope and took a close look at the persona I presented to the companies I had worked for. After polishing the package and learning how to promote it, I mastered human relations skills, such as diplomacy, cooperation, initiative-taking, and networking. I also refined personal development skills, such as organization, time management, and attitude adjustment. Eventually, I overcame the negativity that was making me miserable and holding me back in my career. By my late 20s, I saw results in the form of four promotions, and I could finally claim that I was—at long last—happy working in the corporate world.

Every time I socialize with other young professionals, I realize that my experiences are disturbingly common. We technically have more occupational choices than our parents did, but because the turbulent economy has limited our options, we face escalating uncertainty about our careers. More than ever, twenty-somethings worldwide are seeking counseling, and job jumping due to stress and dissatisfaction has become the norm. For example, recent studies by the U.S. Bureau of Labor Statistics show that the average American holds 8.6 jobs between the ages of 18 and 32, and that the median length of time workers stay in one job has shrunk by half since 1983—from 2.2 years then, to 1.1 years now. Additionally, a 2003 labor study by the Danish Social Science Research Council found that the average person in Denmark will have at least 12 different employers by the time they reach the age of 60, and, in 2003, the Australian Human Rights and Equal Opportunity Commission established that 42 percent of their country's workers change jobs at least every two years.

At the end of the day, the choice is yours. You can help NYU Law and Northwestern's Kellogg School of Management increase their applications by another 200 percent while you shell out $100,000 for three or four more years of school. Or, because you don't want to be in debt and eating with plastic utensils the rest of your life, you can learn to win the game of corporate business. Difficult as it may be, you must change your attitude about the education you left behind. A college degree is a piece of paper that gets you in the door for an interview—it may even land you a job. But if you want to get any further in the corporate world, you have to treat your first job out of college like it's 1st grade. This new world is full of possibilities, but you must be willing to readjust your thinking cap and prepare for some tough lessons. And no—most of those lessons can't be learned on *The Apprentice*. Some of those folks broke every rule in business, from dressing down to mouthing off. Their behavior slid by because they were on a reality television show, working for Donald Trump. The rest of us aren't so lucky.

The sad state of the current economy is making the business climate tougher than it has ever been. I came, I saw, and I *didn't* go back to school. That's why I decided to write this book. By sharing the strategies that helped me succeed in my career, I hope to provide a helping hand to those just beginning the journey, and also to reassure those who have been in the trenches for some time already that it is possible to make sense of this upside-down world.

The contents of *They Don't Teach Corporate in College* are as follows: The first chapter serves as the insider's guide to job hunting, including unorthodox (yet proven) techniques for surveying the field, meeting contacts, preparing promotional materials, and interviewing. Chapter 2 will help you transition to a new position, and suggests actions that will help you achieve the best possible first impression. The third chapter lays out strategies for getting to know a new boss, navigating the company's social scene, and practicing cringe-free networking. Chapter 4 describes critical skills such as goal-setting, self-promotion, problem-solving, and risk-taking, which will take you wherever you decide to go. Chapter 5 covers how to stretch the 8-plus hours a day you spend at work—everything from effective time management and organization, to making every piece of communication count.

The sixth chapter is devoted to combating negativity, maintaining a positive attitude, and staying motivated in the face of difficult circumstances. Chapter 7 focuses on approaches for enlisting the cooperation of others, creating positive relationships, and coping with difficult personalities. The eighth chapter is a how-to on advancement, including mastering the performance review process, troubleshooting antipromotion situations, and coping with organizational change. Chapter 9 will guide you through your first experience as a boss, drilling down into specific techniques for starting off on the right foot with your employees, delegating tasks, facilitating open communication, and resolving performance issues. The last chapter advises when it's time to move on, and offers suggestions for finding a new position and making a graceful exit.

What's the best way to use this book? I suggest that you jot down on paper the concepts that resonate with you so that you can remember them later. Post your notes in your cubicle or office—anywhere you'll see them. Some of the ideas mentioned might seem like common sense, but you'd be surprised how rarely people act on them in real life. If at any point you feel like all this is not worth the effort, just consider how much time you are likely to spend in the corporate world. Assuming you work from age 22 to age 65, for 235 days a year, you'll be on someone else's clock for about 80,000 hours—or 1/10 of your life. Isn't it only fair that you do everything you can to create a rewarding job experience?

There's one more thing I want to emphasize before we begin: The strategies I'm about to discuss are "best practices"—that is, they represent the ideal way to handle particular situations. While you should generally stick to these principles if you want to be successful, no one expects you to follow them to the letter every time. As human beings, it's impossible for us to be perfect corporate employees. We can sing self-improvement mantras until we're blue in the face, but at the end of the day we will still have our areas of strength and areas where we can always do better. So don't be too hard on yourself. The best you can do is to read through these 10 chapters and pick out the concepts that you feel you can benefit the most from. If you shut this book and take away one piece of advice that makes you more effective at work, then I will have achieved my purpose in writing it.

Chapter 1

Find Yourself, Find a Paycheck

Whether you're just coming out of school or are mid-career, searching for employment in the corporate world is more challenging than any assignment you'll be given on the job. Not only do you have to decide exactly what to look for, but you also have to find a way in the door and make that doorstop hold until you have an offer in hand. Fortunately, like any game with rules, job hunting has its loopholes. In this chapter, I'll discuss how to take advantage of them as you're surveying the field, meeting contacts, preparing your promotional materials, and interviewing. I'll also touch on the sticky question of money and how you can ask for more when they want to pay you less.

The Panic Button

For me, preparing to enter the corporate world was a lot like being reborn. At the end of my senior year of college, I felt the same sense of discomfort that a baby must feel when leaving the safety of his mother's womb. I freaked out about being unemployed and having to move back home, so I stormed my university's career center and wreaked havoc on every job catalog and database I could get my hands on. I needed a job ASAP, and I was willing to take anything I could get, regardless of whether or not I was interested in the occupation. After all, it was only my first job, right? The media reinforced my belief that because I was 22, I wasn't supposed to have a clue. Alexandra Robbins and Abby Wilner, authors of *Quarterlife Crisis: The Unique Challenges of Life in Your Twenties*, define a quarterlife crisis as the "overwhelming instability, self-doubt, and sense of panicked helplessness faced by twenty-somethings as a result of constant change and too many choices." I became complacent, thinking that because I'd inevitably change my mind a million times, I might as well put off the soul-searching.

Even if this approach seems perfectly legitimate to you, I don't recommend it. First of all, prospective employers don't like unfocused candidates; they want to believe that you've been preparing to work for them forever. Also, switching careers multiple times just for the hell of it sounds like a lot of work to me. You need a lot of training and experience to become proficient in a career, and once you have a family to support, will you be able to afford to pursue the job you love at a $20,000 entry-level salary? Along those same lines, your 20s is the best time to get to a respectable level on the corporate ladder. During these years you don't have competing responsibilities, and you are accountable to no one but yourself.

Given these factors, wouldn't it be much easier to make the smartest career choice you can now? Now don't get me wrong—discovering your true calling is not an exact science, and it's impossible to know what you will want to do 10 or 20 years from now. Some futurists even predict that people our age will have seven different jobs in their lifetimes—four of which haven't been invented yet.

Therefore, all of the self-reflection in the world will probably not result in a bulletproof career plan for the rest of your life. It's also possible that you will try a field you've researched and think is interesting, but will realize you hate it after a few months on the job. However, by doing a complete self-assessment while you're still in school or shortly thereafter, you will be able to decide on a path that provides the core skills and experience you will need to take you wherever you want to go in the future.

The Self-Assessment Journey

Start with a blank slate. This is easier said than done when everyone you know, especially your parents, has an opinion on what you should do now that you're all grown up. You also have to get past the issue of your major. You might think that because you studied economics, you have to pursue a career as a financial consultant. The truth is that even a business-related major will not adequately prepare you for the corporate world, so why let it pigeonhole you?

Forget what you studied in school for a moment and make a list of your skills—otherwise known as the things you do better than most of your friends. Skills can be *general* or *specific*. (An example of a general skill is communicating well with people, and an example of a corresponding specific skill is that you present well in front of groups.) Next, sit down for a brief philosophical journey and reflect on the following questions:

- What are your values?
- What type of work would make you want to sit in traffic for hours just for the privilege of showing up? What would you be compelled to do even if you never got paid for it?

- How do you prefer to work? How are you most effective?
- What is your definition of success? What drives you?
- Where do you see yourself in 10 years?

Use the answers to these questions to develop what Stephen Covey, author of *The 7 Habits of Highly Effective People*, calls a "personal mission statement." To paraphrase Covey, the *personal mission statement* is your own big picture. It should include what you hope to accomplish in your career and reflect the type of person you want to become. By thinking about what's really important to you and where you want to go in life, your efforts and energy will be directed toward a common purpose. Along with your list of skills, your personal mission statement should provide clues about fields to research.

Now hit the library or the Internet and pore over reference material about occupations that correspond to your skills, interests, and personal mission. Once you've made a list of potential careers, ask the career center at your college or university to help you set up informational interviews with alumni so that you can learn more about each job field you are interested in. In these meetings, don't be afraid to ask specific questions about training requirements, responsibilities, salary, work environment, and opportunities for advancement. As long as you are polite, no one will fault you for wanting the real scoop. Plus, if a job is not as glamorous as it sounds, you will want to know that before investing more of your time and energy. If possible, sample your options by taking courses related to the careers that interest you, applying for internships in your target occupations, or visiting prospective companies so that you can get a real feel for the field you'll be pursuing.

If you've already been in the business world a few years, I suggest a healthy reality check before you jump over to another job. Revise or develop your personal mission statement and ask yourself if you're on the right track. Why aren't you happy in your current position? Is it your career choice, your work situation, or you? If it's the second or third scenario, read on. Hopefully this book will help you. If it's your career choice, though, this might be a good time to make an appointment with a career counselor, take a personality inventory such as the Myers-Briggs Type Indicator, or read a career assessment book such as *What Color Is Your Parachute?* by Richard Nelson Bolles (Ten Speed Press, 2003). Even if you're mid-career, you can still find a job that works for you.

When you've collected enough data to make an informed decision about a particular field, imagine your career path over the next five or 10 years. Suppose you land a dream job in your chosen field. You'll want to set some preliminary goals for what you hope to accomplish once you get there. In determining aspirations and time frames, try to be realistic. The dot-com boom is over, and if your objective is to be a millionaire by age 30, you are setting yourself up for disappointment. (For more information on setting goals, see Chapter 4.) You should also have a backup plan. What will you do if you can't find a job or you don't succeed in your first career choice? Knowing you have something to fall back on will only increase your confidence level as you hold your nose and dive in.

No matter what direction you choose, you'll have to cope with some doubt and uncertainty. But don't let indecisiveness get the best of you. Staying unemployed for too long while you consider the perfect career move will drive you crazy and make prospective employers squirm. Make the best decision you can, act confidently, and never look back. If you do what you think is best, the pieces will most likely fall into place.

Your Corporate Persona

> The semester before I graduated, I flew home to look for a job. I had been kind of lazy in college, and my parents didn't feel I was ready for the corporate world. They even told me to hold off on interviewing. I didn't listen, though. I bought a new suit, got a haircut, and practiced by talking to myself in the mirror for a week. When I went in to meet with employers, I pretended like I'd been a smooth professional all my life. My parents met me for dinner one night, and they kept looking for traces of the former bum. I think they were in shock. My dad was like, 'Well, I guess maybe you are ready.'
>
> Dan, 27, Rhode Island

In life, we get many chances to reinvent ourselves. Remember when you first arrived on campus for your freshman year of college? The most exciting thing about it was that no one knew what a (*insert negative adjective of choice here*) you were in high school. You taught yourself new habits and hobbies, and you bought yourself a new wardrobe. Maybe you even picked a new nickname. You had the chance to start over, as if your previous life had never been.

Graduating from college is a similar opportunity, and, understandably, you probably want to spend the next few years figuring out who you are and what you want out of life. Should you decide to pursue a career in business, however, developing a *corporate persona* will unquestionably serve you well. By corporate persona, I mean the mature, professional, and competent face you project to the work world. It doesn't matter what type of person you are in real life, just think of yourself as an actor playing a role while you are at work. So what if you still play drinking games on Friday nights or prefer a book to human company? You can still have a corporate persona.

How will this help you? Quite simply, a marketable persona positively influences people's perceptions of you so that you can ultimately succeed in the corporate world. I'm sure you've heard of big-time publicists who get paid megabucks to promote celebrities and make them look like the coolest people on earth. You can be just like those PR folks, only you have just one client to promote—*you*. It's pretty easy, but there is a catch: You must first learn to toot your own horn. Although there is a fine line between confidence and arrogance, learning to capitalize on your skills and assert your achievements is a must for career success. If you don't do it, no one else will, and you'll be out-promoted by people who know how to leverage their own contributions. Trust me on this. In the end it will pay off almost as handsomely for you as it does for the wealthiest of publicists.

Growing and maintaining a corporate persona is hard work because everything you say and do affects it one way or the other. The best way to make your persona stick is to clearly establish it at the beginning of your relationship with a company and consistently sustain it during the early phases of a new job. Keeping this idea in mind, let's move on to the mechanics of finding a job.

Scoping the Field

Getting a good job in today's economy requires more than just graduating from a good college and hanging out at recruiting fairs. You have to set yourself apart, get their attention, and make them want you.

You probably don't have a lot of time to make this happen. If you're unemployed, you might be cashing in the last of your savings bonds to make your rent, and you need a job ASAP. If you already have a job and are looking for another, you have only so many hours to inconspicuously surf the Internet before your boss figures out what's going on. When you're in your 20s, employment is a catch 22—you need experience to get a job, but you must have a job in order to get that experience. Our forefathers relied on temp agencies to float them through the job-search process. Unfortunately, we don't have that luxury. These days, temp firms are more crowded than a U2 concert. You'll sit in their plush waiting rooms for hours, filling out personality questionnaires and waiting for a free computer station so you can prove you're Microsoft-compliant.

Don't despair, though. Landing a job in the corporate world is quite achievable with a little ingenuity and preparation. Don't give them a reason to hire you; dare them to find a reason not to. This is where the concept of the corporate persona comes in. Every interaction you have with a company—from your first written communication to your salary negotiation—should exude maturity, professionalism, and competency. You want the employer to say, "Wow, I've never seen a more together candidate. So what if the company is in a hiring freeze? I have to get her on board."

So where do you start? A good first step is to scout out openings commensurate with your level of experience. Here are some places to try:

- Your college career center and/or alumni network.

- Career Websites, such as CareerBuilder.com (*www.careerbuilder.com*), HotJobs (*http://hotjobs.yahoo.com*), and Monster (*www.monster.com*). These are Internet portals where you can post your resume and sign up to receive job openings by e-mail.

- Employment or recruiting agencies—aka *headhunters*, or people who get paid by a company to scout out desirable candidates.

- Company Websites with job postings.

- Searchable databases, such as MonsterTRAK (*www.jobtrack.com*) or America's Job Bank (*www.ajb.dni.us*).

- Local job fairs.

- Trade associations.

- Newspaper want ads.

Keep in mind that most job openings aren't advertised because a lot of businesses prefer to hire from within the company or through word of mouth. If you're coming in from off the street, you could be out of luck. Recently, my friend Jake tore through New York City in search of a job. In a week, he dropped 200 resumes at a career expo, signed with five recruiting firms, and answered dozens of Internet job postings. Boy, was he bitter when he was still unemployed after his month-long assault on the New York job market. Jake learned that, unfortunately, being proactive is sometimes not enough. Instead of working harder, work *smarter*. Use online resources, such as Hoover's (*www.hoovers.com*), and business trade publications, such as *The Wall Street Journal*, *Forbes*, *Fortune*, and *BusinessWeek*, to target desirable companies in your geographic area.

Then, prepare to infiltrate these companies by making the transition from outsider to insider. Here's how:

- Get to know individuals already employed at your target company who are in a position to hire you. (See "The Myth of Cover Letters" on page 28).
- Apply for an internship position that will land you inside the company and provide you with an opportunity to build your skill portfolio.
- Secure referrals from anyone you know in your chosen field—either people with years of experience behind them, such as old professors and your parents' friends, or recent graduates who will have sympathy for your plight and might also be more familiar with a company's lower-level job openings.

Using a combination of these approaches, you are much more likely to gain access to unadvertised job openings in the companies you desire. However, it probably won't happen overnight. Be persistent and don't resort to laziness, even if you're not seeing immediate results. Keep your expectations realistic and remind yourself of the end goal every day. Above all, don't doubt your own abilities. Ignore all of the folks who tell you that the market sucks and that you should take any available job, even if it's not what you want or need. Learn to take rejection with a grain of salt—it's all part of the process. If you take the right action patiently and efficiently, an opportunity will come along that's a good fit for your skill set.

Irresistible Resumes

From the time I was just out of college, employers have told me that I have a terrific resume. If you think this means that my experience has been equally terrific, think again. Hey, when I was applying for my first job, I didn't have any real experience. I imagined the employer scanning the page for something that mattered to him, and realized I had to make my few skills stand out in a way that would immediately grab his attention.

Leanna, 25, California

The purpose of a resume is to land you an interview. Your local bookstore has a million books about the best way to write a resume so you can achieve that goal. In my opinion, though, writing an impressive resume is simple if you keep a few things in mind. First, employers never read a resume in its entirety, and I'm willing to bet that the average resume gets read in about five seconds.

My father once told me that employers like numbers and statistics—hard facts that show how a candidate is directly responsible for making a company more profitable. Now let's be real here. If you're still in your early 20s, the chances are not very good that you are at a high enough level to have sole ownership of a project. However, the chances are excellent that you have had some measurable impact along the way. Did you help with a project that drove company revenue? Was there any piece of that project that you alone were responsible for? Let's examine how this strategy might work for a candidate who is pursuing her first corporate job, and also for someone who has worked in the business world before.

First Corporate Job

Let's say you didn't have corporate internships while you were in college, but you did sell ice cream at Baskin-Robbins for four summers. Maybe, while you were there, you helped the manager execute a campaign to draw in customers from a nearby shopping mall.

Original Statement: Passed out free ice-cream cone coupons at nearby shopping mall.

Power Statement: Designed and distributed "Snack On Us" coupon targeted to mall shoppers, increasing store traffic by 25 percent.

See why the power statement is better? The original statement makes it look as though you were just a passive body handing out coupons, and the reader is probably thinking that anyone could have done that job. The power statement, however, reads like you made a significant contribution to the Baskin-Robbins corporation by creating an innovative marketing campaign. Note that the wording of the power statement is still good even if you didn't make the flyer all by yourself. If you had any creative input whatsoever, saying that you designed it bolsters the perception of ownership. The "Snack On Us" labeling also suggests that you were responsible for branding the campaign. With one statement, you have completely changed the reader's perception of your role from ice-cream shop cashier to small business entrepreneur.

Early Career Move

Suppose you worked as an administrative assistant in a large consulting firm. You were a member of a team that serviced a healthcare account worth $250,000 in monthly fees. Perhaps most of the real account work was left to the senior individuals on the team, but you were responsible for creating and managing the budget spreadsheets.

Original Statement: Created budget spreadsheets for healthcare account.

Power Statement: Managed finances for healthcare account worth $250,000 in monthly fees.

Maybe your contribution to this account was solely administrative. The first statement reads this way. The power statement, however, makes a reader think that you were responsible for managing an enormous amount of company revenue. It says to me that you are extremely trustworthy, and that you have a head for complicated finances.

As you can see, the words you choose to communicate your experience make all the difference in whether your resume is considered average or fantastic. In public relations, we call this strategy "spinning," and if you don't think it will work for you, sleep on it. With a little creativity and positive positioning, the most mundane tidbits of experience can become resume jewels. Here are some other tips that may help your resume through the door:

- Tailor a resume for each field you are pursuing.
- Choose the layout that best suits your situation:
  - *Chronological*: Employment history is arranged by the dates you worked for

particular companies. (Use this format if you're moving within the same field.)

- ○ *Functional*: Employment history is arranged by skills and accomplishments. (Use this format if you're changing careers.)

- Investigate what experience is required for your targeted position, and then illustrate how you fit the bill.

- List titles that accurately reflect your job description, even if they're not official.

- Focus on results rather than responsibilities.

- Use action verbs to qualify achievements (for example, *coordinated* and *evaluated*).

- Include a section for marketable skills (for example, computer and language skills).

- Keep the document to one page.

- Check for typos and inconsistencies in format.

Finally, make sure your resume has up-to-date contact information, including a phone number and e-mail address. If you are going to put your cell phone number on your resume so that you can be reached quickly, don't forget to replace your cutesy greeting with one that is tailored to your most important audience: your potential employer. (See Chapter 5 for voice-mail message tips.)

The Myth of Cover Letters

Burning the midnight oil to write a spectacular cover letter to send with your resume is not the best use of your time. Why? It's critical that the right people read your materials, and that probably won't happen with a traditional cover letter and resume addressed to a human resources manager and sent by snail mail. Your resume could be better than Barbara Walters's, but if it sits on Mr. HR's desk for six months, it's useless. My approach to sending introductory communications may be a little unorthodox, but the results speak for themselves.

Three years ago, when I was looking for a job, I read two resume-writing books cover to cover and proceeded to cut my tongue by licking envelopes for 50 cover letters and resumes. I received form letters from 20 percent of the companies and no response at all from the other 80 percent. Desperate, I tried the following method and got a job offer the first time.

No matter what the recruiters say, e-mail is the best way to communicate with the individual who can hire you. It's easier than you think. The first step is to ask everyone you talk to if they know someone at your target company. Inevitably, you'll be chatting with someone at a party and will find out that her sister-in-law works for "Fab Company." Should you find yourself in this situation, don't waste time reflecting on the coincidental nature of the world. It's your lucky day! Get the contact's name and ask your new best friend if she'd mind if you e-mailed her sister-in-law. She'll probably say yes to your request, because most people like to help someone out. Be sure to thank her profusely. Then go home right away and draft a cordial e-mail resembling the following example. Mention the name of the family member that you met at the party in the subject line so that your contact will open the message instead of deleting it with her spam. The tone of the message should not be wishy-washy or vague. Keep it short and sweet, ask for what you want up front, and be specific.

Subject: Referred by Jenny Partygoer

Dear Ms. Sister-in-Law:

I'm a friend of your sister-in-law, Jenny Partygoer. Jenny mentioned that you worked at Fab Company, and I'm hoping you could offer me some advice. I'm looking for a new position in my field of expertise, and I believe that Fab Company might be a good fit for my skills and experience. Do you think you could put me in touch with someone in the Widget Creation Department of your company who might be willing to have a look at my resume? Thanks so much.

Sincerely yours,
Jill Jobhunter

So what happens if you've shouted Fab Company's name from the rooftops and you still can't make a connection to someone who works there? The situation is not hopeless by any means, but you will have to do a little more digging. Call around and look on the Internet to find the names of people who work in your proposed department. You don't need to locate a senior manager—anybody with a similar job function will do. Find out as much about the person as you can, and then craft a short, friendly e-mail introducing yourself and explaining what you're looking for. Don't worry about e-mailing a total stranger about job opportunities. Many companies offer finder's fees to employees for recommending potential hires, and if your contact will receive money if they hire you, he'll want to help if he can. Here's an example:

Subject: Your press release on Fabcompany.com

Dear Mr. Smith:

I noticed that you handle Widget PR for Fab Company, and I was hoping you could offer me some advice. As I will be relocating to Atlanta this fall, I'm interested in exploring potential career opportunities with your firm. I am a marketing communications executive with four years of experience promoting Widgets (resume attached), and I believe my skills and experience would be a good fit for your company. Any feedback you could provide would be greatly appreciated. Thanks so much.

Sincerely yours,
Jill Jobhunter

Even if Mr. Smith is not the person who would ask you in for an interview, you've now made it inside the company. Mr. Smith probably has the internal contacts to introduce you to the person who can hire you. Perhaps he will forward your information directly, or mention to several of his colleagues that you'll be contacting them.

Even if you can obtain an important person's phone number, I wouldn't call until you've exchanged a few communications via e-mail. For one thing, the chances of getting a higher-level executive on the phone are pretty slim. If the exec doesn't know you, getting past her assistant will be like robbing a casino. Also, leaving a voice-mail message has the unsavory intrusiveness of a cold sales call. In the beginning, stick to e-mail—it really is your best opportunity to knock the socks off someone who matters.

Polished Interviews

I left my last job under pretty dismal circumstances. HR had failed to settle an ongoing dispute between my boss and me, so I quit. I was so depressed and unmotivated, I thought of leaving the corporate world for good. But then I got an interview opportunity at a really prestigious company in the city, so I dusted off my resumes and went. My interviewer and I bonded immediately. We had been talking for about a half hour when she asked me why I left my last job. She was so nice and understanding that I felt perfectly comfortable telling her everything. I didn't regret it until I got the letter telling me they were hiring someone else.

Olivia, 23, Missouri

The key to stress-free interviewing is to prepare, but not too much. You want to do just enough research so that you know what to expect and can speak intelligently on the points related to your job function. It helps to jot down a few "wow 'em" facts about the company that you would never know unless you did your homework. However, don't spend too much time on the company's Website that you end up sounding like an encyclopedia in the interview.

It's in your best interest to find out as much as you can about the person or people interviewing you so that you know who you're dealing with. An Internet search might prove helpful in this regard. Determine in advance what type of interview you'll be having so that you aren't caught off guard. Will the meeting be one-on-one, or will you be sitting in front of a panel of executives? Will you be asked to consider a real-life business problem? Will any type of written or computer test be required while you're there?

If your past experience can be demonstrated on paper, I recommend putting together an interview portfolio. A portfolio is a three-ring binder in which you can include anything that highlights your business achievements and shows your level of commitment to previous positions. For example, I'm a marketing communications executive, so my portfolio includes press releases and business plans I've written, magazine articles I've contributed to, and print advertising campaigns I've helped develop. A neat and professional portfolio can be an excellent tool to refer to during an interview. Most people don't bother to create one, but it speaks volumes about your ability to package yourself.

While it's a good idea to be conversational during an interview, be careful how much personal information you divulge. There is never a good reason to bad-mouth your previous employer, even if everything you say is justified. While he is listening to your sob story, your prospective employer is thinking how in a year you will be sitting in front of another interviewer complaining about *his* company. Don't be fooled by an interviewer that seems compassionate. Remember, the two of you are not friends, and that the interviewer's first loyalty is to the company he's hiring for. If you are asked why you left a job, answer with a neutral statement, such as "The commute didn't allow me to spend enough time with my family" or "I wanted to gain experience working in a different industry." Here are some other things to keep in mind as you undergo the interview process:

Pre-Interview

- Familiarize yourself with basic interview questions, such as "Tell me about yourself?" Don't forget doozy interview questions, such as "What is your worst quality?"

- Assess your own skills and career path in the context of the position.

- Brainstorm three to five of your most important business accomplishments and practice succinctly communicating the challenges and results of each one.

- Think of some appropriate questions of your own to ask the interviewer.

- Be careful not to memorize your comments so that they end up sounding scripted.

The Day of the Interview

- Dress in neat, formal business attire.
- Don't arrive too early or too late.
- Carry a nice briefcase that looks worn, but not too worn.
- Begin with a strong handshake.
- Speak confidently, even if you feel like hurling from nervousness.
- Avoid talking nonstop without taking time to listen sincerely.
- Refrain from saying anything negative.
- Pay attention to nonverbal cues—yours and the interviewer's.
- Take a moment to think, if you don't know an answer immediately.
- Let the interviewer bring up the topic of money first.

After the Interview

- Write thank-you notes to everyone you spoke to.

- Follow up with the interviewer for a status on your offer.

The Real Deal

My first job out of college was at a sporting equipment manufacturer. That kind of place attracts a lot of 'jocks' and wannabe 'jocks.' I came into that environment as the smart kid from a good school, and these people felt it was their right to harass me as much as they wanted. I really couldn't relate to my coworkers because they were all married with children. Also, for them, it was just a job, and I was genuinely interested in the technology I was working with. It was a terrible fit. I didn't know until I left that job that the workplace does not have to be like that. At my new company, I found people with similar interests and was able to enjoy my work much more.

Frank, 28, Florida

Many companies have their human resources representatives conduct interviews, but you should try to meet with—or at least speak with—the person who will be your official manager. The reason behind this is pretty simple: If your personalities clash or if you have fundamental differences in the way you work, you need to know immediately so that you can determine if you want to pursue the opportunity further. I'm not saying that one conversation will accurately reflect how your boss will act on the job or that problems won't arise later that were impossible to predict. However, if you hate the person on sight, you should consider if it's a smart move to work for her.

While you're interviewing, you should also talk to existing employees at the company—preferably those in the department you want to work for. Tactfully learn as much as you can about the *corporate culture*, or the working environment and the politics of the company. Think seriously about whether you could fit in, because you won't be able to have a happy and fruitful career in a company that makes you uncomfortable or doesn't meet your individual needs. Get a sense of the overall mood and morale of the employees, and listen carefully to what they say—and what they *don't* say. If you think that every employee is going to sing the company's praises just because you came up from HR, you might be surprised. I interviewed at a technology company that really impressed me until two of my potential colleagues told me to leave "before I got sucked in." I didn't take the offer, but I might have if I hadn't taken the time to get the insider's view.

A quick word about interview thank-you notes: Some people think e-mail thank-you letters are enough, but I have to disagree. If you want the company to think you are a "go the extra mile" type of person, start by spending the extra minute it takes to snail mail actual cards.

Airtight References

You just had a successful interview, the employer is about to make you an offer, and then he asks for a few references to reassure himself that he wants to hire you. The operative word here is *reassure*. By the time employers get to the reference stage, their minds are usually made up, and they are just doing their due diligence. That said, you must assume that your references will be called and, subsequently, grilled about your work experience. So, yes, your references have to be real people, and the contact information you provide for them must be accurate and up-to-date.

The best references are not your best friend's mother or your favorite elementary school teacher. They also do not include your current boss. I don't care how chummy the two of you are—you don't want your manager to know you're looking for another position. If you've never had a job before, you might ask an internship supervisor or a professor you've worked with to be a reference. If you have been employed, a friend you worked with in the past or a former boss from a job you left under good circumstances are good choices.

Do not give out references' names and contact information without talking to them first. Actually, you should contact potential references at the beginning of your job search and debrief each one on the types of opportunities you're looking for. If they agree to be references, speak to them again immediately after you've given their names to an employer. Let them know that the employer is going to call, and make sure to give them as many specifics about the position as you can. Is there an aspect of your personality, background, or experience that your references should emphasize in order to better your chances? If so, be sure to tell them. Providing your references with the key points you want them to mention will make it easier for them to help you.

Follow up with your references to determine if the employer called them. If they were called, get the 411 on the conversations, and then send each reference a thank-you note. If they weren't, don't freak out. I've heard of employers who ask for references just to make sure you have them—they have no intention of actually speaking with anyone. At any rate, send your references thank-you notes whether they were called or not. You never know when you might need them again.

One last point: It's not necessary to put "References Available Upon Request" on the bottom of your resume. Believe me, if an employer needs references in order to hire you, she'll ask for them.

Negotiation Prowess

The key to a successful salary negotiation is to avoid getting screwed, and to come out smelling like a rose in the process. You also want to make sure you get the most money possible up front, because once you are inside a company, increases are few and far between. In order to make this happen, you need to plan ahead. Before you go on an interview, you should have a good idea of what you—and the target job—are worth. If you've just graduated from college, you might not have much choice but to accept whatever entry-level salary the firm pays. If you're scouting for a new job, however, you should check Internet salary sites to see how much you can command given your level of expertise, your geographic location, and your years of experience. Next, call the target company's human resources department to find out the salary range of the available position. Finally, David Gordon, Internship Director of the Marketing Communications Department at Columbia College of Chicago, suggests a few questions to ask yourself prior to discussing your salary with a prospective employer:

- Are my personal salary requirements in line with the company's range for this position? If not, is there a chance to get more money?
- What is the lowest salary I will consider?
- What makes me worth more than what they are offering?

Gordon also notes that you should prepare for objections to your request for more money, including 1) you don't have enough experience, 2) other employees at your level aren't making that much, 3) the budget won't permit it, and 4) that's what they are paying new hires. Think about how you would respond to these objections in a way that continues the discussion on a positive note. Prepare to phrase your comments in the form of questions, keeping in mind that the end goal is to reach an agreement that both parties are happy with.

As I mentioned before, try not to be the first one to mention money in the interview, and avoid giving your salary range, if possible. When the interviewer asks you about your salary, keep your response vague, or ask what the company has budgeted for the position. If you must reveal what you're currently making, inflate the number slightly to account for bonuses, perks, or if you're due for a raise shortly. You should never lie outright about your salary, though, as some companies may require a job applicant to submit a pay stub.

After the employer makes an offer, remember to ask about other benefits that might add weight, such as stock options, bonuses, and vacation time. If you're happy with the total package, communicate that to the employer, and ask him if you can have 24 hours to consider it. Next, politely ask for the offer in writing. If you feel you need to negotiate for a higher salary, tread carefully. Gordon advocates the following techniques:

- Reinforce how much you want to work for the company.
- Put a human face on the situation.
- Mention that other opportunities will pay your desired salary.

For example, you might say, "I'm really excited about this position and I think I'm a great fit for the company, but I don't think I could afford to take less than my minimum of $45,000. I have several other opportunities that are in my range, but I'd really prefer to work for you. Is there any way we could work this out?"

Remember that salary ranges are rarely fixed, and once the interviewer has decided she wants to hire you, she will usually meet your request for more money. However, occasionally you might find that great career moves come with a lower price tag. You might be wise to accept an offer that is less money initially, yet pays greater dividends in terms of growth and experience.

Chapter 1 Take Home Points

✓ **Explore your career options.** Before putting yourself on the job market, take the time to fully investigate career options that will utilize your skills, interests, and personal mission.

✓ **Promote yourself.** Think of yourself as a publicist with the task of promoting *you*. Learn to capitalize on your skills and succinctly assert your achievements.

✓ **Learn to network.** Don't base your job search solely on advertised openings. Increase your chances of landing interviews by personally connecting with individuals within your target companies.

✓ **Create a corporate persona.** Project a *corporate persona* (your most mature, professional, and competent face) throughout the job search, application, interview, and negotiation processes.

Chapter 2

Congratulations, You're Hired

What a relief. Your job search is officially over. You've accepted an offer and have agreed to start the following Monday. Resist the urge to become complacent. Between now and the end of your first month on the job, it is critical that you skillfully wield your corporate persona to make a stellar impression. While it may sound intimidating, transitioning into a new work situation is fairly easy once you know what you need to do. This chapter will walk you through the actions you should take prior to your start date and during your first few weeks on the new job. Here I'll also cover some new-employee essentials that will help you be successful, such as decoding office lingo and getting past human resources.

The Start Before the Start

Maybe you're thinking, "There's nothing I can do until I actually get there, right?" Not true. If you didn't interview with the person who will be your immediate supervisor, contact her immediately. Send an introductory e-mail, and while you're at it, ask her if she has any materials you can review that will better prepare you for your first day. Has your new company been in the news lately? Include a line in your letter that shows you've been keeping up. This short note will probably take 10 minutes to compose and will do wonders for your boss's preliminary perception of you as a competent and proactive new hire.

If your manager sends materials, be sure to read them carefully. Common sense, right? Well, sad to say, I was caught with my pants down when, on my first day of a new job, my manager asked me a question about the annual report he'd mailed. I'd only skimmed the report and didn't have it in front of me, so I choked. Hopefully you are a better BS-er than me, but knowing the facts can never hurt—especially in a new work situation. Also, if your new manager mentions any important team meetings or conference calls that will take place before your first day, volunteer to join them via telephone. This might be difficult to do when you're still sitting at your desk in your old company, but try to swing it if you can. Your new colleagues will be impressed to see you involved before you're on the company's clock, and, next thing you know, everyone on the team will be looking forward to your start date.

Camille Lavington, a personal marketing consultant and author of *You've Only Got Three Seconds*, says that when you first meet someone, you only have three seconds to make an indelible impression. The moment an individual sees you, he evaluates your clothing, hairstyle, grooming habits, facial cues, and posture. Without even thinking about it, he'll decide whether he wants to get to know you better and whether you are worthy of being taken seriously. No matter what you say from that point on, his opinion of you will be heavily influenced by his initial perception. Three seconds is not a lot of time. Plus, during your first day at a new job, you will meet a lot of people who are important to your future success. You will also have to cope with one major disadvantage that you can't do anything about—your age. Even if you alter your appearance or demeanor, you will probably still look like a twenty-something. Some people will expect you to act flaky or immature because you are young, and the burden is on you to prove them wrong. Needless to say, you'll want to prepare for these challenges before you arrive.

Looking the Part

Let's start here. Like it or not, most of the corporate world is conservative at heart. On your first day, show up wearing a clean and neatly tailored suit, even if the rest of the company dresses in business casual. You might be over-dressed, but I guarantee no one will criticize you for it. Rather, your colleagues will respect that you mean business, and your boss will be proud to introduce you around the company. Besides, isn't it easier to act professionally when you look the part? I know that when I'm sitting down to a meeting and I'm wearing khakis, I sometimes forget to cross my legs. I never make that mistake when I'm wearing a suit. If your company is business casual, you can taper off the suit-wearing after a few weeks. However, if the dress is mixed (some wear formal business attire, others business casual), I suggest staying with the suit. You'll be able to compete with the best-dressed people in the company, you'll appear older, and you'll look like a million bucks when you run into the CEO in the elevator. A colleague once told me that if I dressed like the VPs, I would become one faster because people would be able to picture me in a higher position.

I've also heard that women primarily look at shoes and jewelry when evaluating other women. Don't have a lot of money? I recommend investing in three good pairs of dress shoes and a few pieces of simple, but high-quality gold jewelry. The best advice I have for guys is to shave often and wear ties that don't scream for attention. And forgive me for saying this, but lose any visible body piercings. I know it's not fair, but the fact is that a man wearing an earring has a certain connotation in the corporate world. Save it for the weekends. Something that tiny should not be allowed to compromise your corporate persona.

Meeting and Greeting

The day I started a new job in event planning, my department was preparing for our annual conference in Philadelphia. We were on our hands and knees stuffing customer information packets the whole day, and by 7 p.m., my new suit was impossibly wrinkled, my stockings had a run, and I was flustered beyond belief. My boss told me our Group Head wanted to meet me, so I made a quick pit stop at the bathroom to freshen up and calm myself down. I took a deep breath and walked confidently into the Group Head's office, smiling and looking as relaxed as if I was on a cruise. Later, my boss told me that the Group Head was really impressed with me. I asked how this was possible, considering he had just met me, and my boss said that the Group Head felt that anyone who could be so together after such an insane first day must be a good find. That brief interaction set a positive tone for my relationship with the big boss from that point forward.

Marisol, 29, Maryland

Your first week at a new job will be a whirlwind of new people and situations. When I jumped from an office with 300 people to one with more than 3,000, I was so confused, I had trouble remembering *anyone's* name for a few weeks. Nevertheless, as I mentioned previously, the first few moments of interaction between you and other people will shape their appraisal of you. So when you are introduced to new colleagues, remember to make eye contact, smile, and shake their hands firmly. Ask them their names, and find out what they do for the company. Jot these things down quickly, along with anything else that might help you remember them. Engage in small talk freely if the conversation goes that way, staying away from thorny political issues that could get you into trouble. Show that you are interested in them by paying them sincere compliments or asking appropriate personal questions.

In these first conversations, the goal is to project enthusiasm, confidence, and an aura of respect—no matter who you're meeting. I've seen new people come into a company and put their best face on for the executives, while disregarding everyone else. This is not smart. A corporate persona is nothing if not consistent. Besides, you won't know who the company influencers are at the beginning. It's a good bet to pay special attention to administrative assistants. These individuals tend to have the executives' ears, and they know how to work the system. When meeting or dealing with "admins," be polite or even deferential. They may turn out to be the most important allies you have in the company.

If your manager doesn't send an e-mail welcoming you to the department, it's a nice gesture for you to introduce yourself this way. The message should be no more than a few lines containing a brief summary of your background and stating how happy you are to be working there. Create an e-mail signature, and add it to your outgoing messages so that your colleagues can note your full name, title, and contact information.

Decoding Office Lingo

If you thought everyone in the corporate world spoke your language, think again. The business world's language is one of subtlety, filled with euphemisms and pet phrases to cleverly disguise what people actually mean. Because you wouldn't visit a foreign country without a pocket translator, I've provided one here for your convenience that covers office lingo. Study these basic phrases at the beginning of your journey, and you'll be talking like a native in no time.

1. Phrase: *"I've got too much on my plate."*
What it means: This person has too much work to do or is trying to look like she has too much work to do, so someone else will have to take on any new assignments.

2. Phrase: *"I just wanted to close the loop."*
What it means: This person has made progress on an issue you were involved in and is, thankfully, keeping you informed.

3. Phrase: *"Let's assess the team's bandwidth."*
What it means: This person is trying to find out how much work everyone has to do, probably so she can delegate a new assignment to the person who is least busy.

4. Phrase: *"You and I are not on the same page."*
What it means: This person does not agree with you or there is a communication breakdown regarding the best way to proceed with a project.

5. Phrase: *"I'm in crisis mode."*
What it means: The person is stressed about a matter that may or may not be urgent. Either way, she does not want to be bothered.

6. Phrase: *"I'm just calling to touch base."*

What it means: This person wants to give you an update on a project or needs to ask you to do something for her.

7. Phrase: *"Don't forget to CYA."* (aka *"Cover Your Ass"*)

What it means: This person wants you to take action to ensure that you are not blamed for something.

8. Phrase: *"FYI...."* (aka *"For Your Information"*)

What it means: This person is indicating to you that you will be held accountable for whatever information she is about to impart.

9. Phrase: *"We're going to have to think outside the box."*

What it means: This person has received instructions from higher up to make sure that a great deal of thought goes into a project, and the pressure is on you to come up with something creative that is different from what has always been done.

10. Phrase: *"Someone dropped the ball."*

What it means: This person is absolving responsibility for a failing project and is implicating someone else on the team. Hopefully the "someone else" isn't you.

11. Phrase: *"You're on the fast track."*

What it means: This person is telling you that you have great potential and will probably be promoted quickly.

12. Phrase: *"Better keep this on your radar screen."*

What it means: This person is implying that she plans to forget what she is about to tell you as soon as the words come out of her mouth. You, on the other hand, are responsible for keeping it top of mind and following up appropriately.

13. Phrase: *"Let's leverage this best practice to add value and impact our bottom line."*

What it means: Whoa, a quadruple whammy! You'll usually

find jargon-filled sentences like these in strategic documents, such as business plans. For simplicity's sake, let's break this one down:

> *Leverage* = recycle previous work
> *Best practice* = how everyone else is doing it
> *Add value* = justify a program's existence
> *Impact bottom line* = make money

So in other words: "We must take advantage of the fact that someone has already come up with a working concept that everyone in the company buys into. You should use this concept to convince the higher-ups that your project will make the company money."

Settling In

> When I showed up to my new office, there was a problem with my Internet connection, and I couldn't get my system up and running for the entire week. I was actually pretty annoyed, but there was no way in hell I was going to show it. I called the help desk a thousand times, and because I was always polite and grateful, I ended up being good friends with the guy. Now, whenever I have a computer issue, I know I'll be his first priority.
>
> Micah, 23, Texas

Imagine being shown to your new office—a windowless cubicle. A dead plant is there to greet you, along with crumbs of dirt all over the carpet. The telephone cord is hopelessly tangled and you don't see a computer anywhere. Welcome to the corporate world! Don't be offended that your new company didn't take the time to set up a nice workspace for you—just move on. The first thing to do (after cleaning up the dirt and setting up your computer, of course) is to get your phone and computer systems in working order so that people can get in touch with you immediately. Providing for the electronic health of your cube is also a good exercise to find out who takes care of such things in the company. Once your voice mail is functional, leave a short, friendly, and professional greeting. Speak slowly and block out as much background noise as possible.

Next, it's time to get some office supplies, so make your way over to the admin's desk. Proceed with caution. No matter what level in the company you are, do not assume that it is the admin's responsibility to order your supplies. Ask her how you can order them, and see what she says. Pouting if you have to do it yourself is not a good idea. Look at it this way—at least now you can get those nifty red folders you like!

Hooray, now it's time to decorate! Just keep in mind that while your cube or office is the space you work in, it belongs to the company. It's fine to place a few framed photographs on your desk and/or pictures on the walls, but don't overdo it. Put all other personal items, including personal paperwork, in a single desk drawer that you can lock at night. You never know when your boss will need something from you after hours, and will take it upon himself to come looking for it. Also, be careful how much food you keep in your cube or office. Laugh if you want, but you don't want to be the one blamed for the mouse that sends 30 colleagues screaming into the hallway.

Plan strategically how you want to organize your desk. I know a lot of people who believe that having a cyclone of a desk makes them look like they are so busy that they just can't keep up with the work raining down on them. That may be true, but it also makes them look terribly disorganized. Being neat and efficient is part of your corporate persona, so even if you're the brilliant "absent-minded professor" type, you might want to modify your habits. Create practical online and offline filing systems that allow easy access to regular materials and can be used readily should a coworker need to take over a project. Remove documents from your mailbox and e-mail inbox as soon as you are finished with them, and write notes in a book or on a dry-erase board to avoid a sticky-pad explosion. I think you'll find that keeping order is easy if you start at the beginning, before reams of paperwork are flooding your desk.

Espionage

Whether you're thrown headfirst into a project or left alone to stare at the walls of your cubicle, the most important thing you can do at the beginning of a new job is to pay attention. You don't have to be a CIA operative to harness the power of smart observation. Simply keep your eyes and ears open, and you will become an expert at mastering the corporate culture of which you are now a part. I know you're eager to let the company know who you are and what you're all about, but keep in mind that the most successful employees are the ones who effectively assimilate into their company's culture.

Do your best to lay low in the beginning. Take the time to study every aspect of your new company, including how people present themselves, how they work together, and how they interact with executives, managers, and clients. What are the written and unwritten rules of engagement? It's particularly useful to watch how employees conduct noncompany business during the workday so that you can get a sense of how personal breaks, e-mail, and phone calls will be tolerated. As you learn, begin to adapt your behavior and work style to suit the work environment.

Examine your company's Website, annual report, and recruiting materials for clues about its mission, goals, image, and values. Is your company more focused on forging ahead in the market or delivering superior customer service? Is the culture guided by competition or cooperation? Is it more important for employees to be solely focused on hard-core business realities or to be well-rounded in their professional and personal lives? If these things are difficult to determine through written materials, you may need to scope out your work area. On my first day at a *Fortune* 500 company, for example, I noticed a book of photographs on my boss's desk. The book, which my company had produced, featured pictures of children in the on-site daycare center. The following week, area schools were closed. I was not surprised to see my colleagues bringing their children into work for a company-sponsored holiday camp. In no time at all, I had become aware of the importance of family in their corporate culture.

Remember that although the corporate world is the same in many ways, cultures vary dramatically from company to company. Just because it was perfectly acceptable to order snacks for an afternoon brainstorming session at your old place of business doesn't mean that your new boss will consider this to be a legitimate expense. Developing a good understanding of your new company's culture will unquestionably serve you well as you look for ways to make a contribution.

Operating the HR Machine

> The first time I had to fill out a W-2 form, I had
> no idea what I was doing. I was too embarrassed
> to ask about it at orientation, so I just fudged it.
> Unfortunately, come tax time, I owed the gov-
> ernment a whole lot of money because I had mis-
> takenly put down that I had a dependent. I wasn't
> planning on this expense at all and I ended up
> having to borrow money from my parents.
>
> Brian, 22, Louisiana

When you're grooming your corporate persona for a
multitude of new colleagues and spying on the company
culture, doing right by human resources may seem like
the least of your challenges. If you're tempted to think
about it this way, just remember that HR hired you, and
they also have the power to make trouble for you, if so
inclined. Learning the ropes early in your career with a
company won't take much time, but it will inevitably save
you major headaches later on.

The New Hire Folder

On your first day, you will probably be asked to fill out
a "Hello, My Name Is" sticker and show up to an orientation for new hires. This event will typically feature overly
enthusiastic guest speakers, generic orientation videos, and
a tedious page-by-page review of a mountain of paperwork.
You will leave the building at the end of the day, head
spinning, with an information packet. Your first instinct

might be to toss it in the dumpster on the way to your car. But, instead, you must take the folder home and reread every word. HR has probably asked you to immediately sign a few legal documents, one of which is a tax form that the company needs in order to pay you. It's important to understand what these documents say, so ask your parents or a friend to help you if you have to. Getting these documents back to HR the next day will serve several purposes: You won't lose or forget about them, your assimilation into the company community will be hassle-free, you will look like a responsible and efficient employee to the "Job Gods" in HR, and you will erase any chance of anyone going to your boss in order to collect your delinquent paperwork.

The new hire folder often includes an employee handbook that outlines company policies, such as initial performance review periods, compensation, dress code, smoking and drugs, sexual harassment, and company benefits. Treat this book like it's your new best friend for a few days. Don't leave it on the train, and avoid the urge to stuff it in a desk drawer without reading it. True story: My friend Zach, who worked for a *Fortune* 500 telecommunications company, was fired after an HR representative caught him smoking on company grounds. Zach was outside the building at the time, but his company had a zero tolerance smoking policy, which was covered in the employee handbook. Although his company's reaction was extreme, Zach was dismissed legally and couldn't do anything about it. The best way to steer clear of these situations is to know where you stand from the get-go.

The Perks

Time Off

Fewer aspects of your job are as important as the number of days you get to spend away from it. That said, you should read and understand your vacation policy up front. Many companies give a standard two weeks per year for new employees, but policies on personal days, paid holidays, sick and bereavement leave, and short-term and long-term disability leave vary. Some businesses also limit the amount of vacation time you can take during your first few months of employment. I accepted my first corporate job six weeks before my college graduation, and, lo and behold, two days before I was scheduled to take off for the ceremony, I ran into a snag with HR because I hadn't cleared unauthorized vacation days ahead of time. By the way, unless you do not have any other choice, don't plan any vacations during your first three months with a company. Remember your corporate persona and consider how jetting off to the Caribbean within weeks of your start date will look to company veterans who haven't taken a vacation in two years.

Medical Benefits

In our 20s, we're accustomed to abusing our bodies and getting away with it. Given that we never get sick and think we're going to live forever, it's easy to take health benefits for granted. However, because group insurance plans are notoriously complicated, it's in your best interest to scope out the lay of the land in case you urgently need a health service. Familiarize yourself with the benefits you are entitled to and make sure you review your coverage in depth before heading to the doctor's or dentist's office. Trust me, it's well worth your time, because once you make a claim the insurance people decline to cover, squabbling with them quickly becomes a frustrating and time-consuming process. Also, playing tug-of-war with an HMO during office hours or inviting your HR benefits administrator to referee are not optimal strategies for minding your professional reputation.

Financial Benefits

Are there ways your company will contribute to your care and feeding beyond the bimonthly paycheck? Yes, indeed. Most companies offer a 401(k), which allows employees to contribute a portion of tax-free income to a savings account. The company will also match a percentage of your contribution, which you get to keep if you stay there an allotted period of time. I could devote an entire book to a discussion about 401(k) plans, but instead I'll share a few tips for leaving your financial future in the hands of your new company:

- Pay close attention to the instructions for rolling over your retirement funds from one company's 401(k) plan to the next. Because you will likely have several jobs during the course of your career, you want your hard-earned savings to transition smoothly.
- Most plans offer a variety of fund distribution options, so you should avoid placing 100 percent of your savings in your company's stock. In these uncertain times, your financial future should not depend on your company's stability.
- Find out how long you have to be employed with a company in order to be *vested,* or qualified to receive a percentage of your company's contribution to your retirement fund. This piece of data could make a difference when deciding whether to stay with a company three full years or two years and 11 months.

If you work for a *public company* (a corporation that issues shares of stock to members of the general public), you might be lucky enough to get stock options. A stock option gives an employee the right to buy or sell shares of company stock at a specific price for a specific period of time. You can typically get an excellent deal on your company's stock by exercising options—but tread carefully. Some employee stock purchase plans have stringent requirements for exercising options, including narrow windows during which you can buy or sell your stock.

Expense Reports

You might think this one is a no-brainer. You spend money on behalf of your company, and then HR pays you back, right? Unfortunately, corporate expense reimbursement can be fraught with peril. On the one hand, you want to get what's owed you. On the other hand, you must also care for your reputation by keeping company expenses down. Because navigating most expense report software programs is a chore, get to know your company's tools before you have items to submit. You should also find out early if corporate expenses must be charged on a particular credit card, or if you are required to use certain vendors in order to be reimbursed. When traveling or eating out on the company's dollar, choose the middle-of-the-road option instead of the most expensive. Most importantly, don't pad your expense reports. Read your policy in detail to determine what you will be reimbursed for, and don't submit anything that doesn't meet these requirements. And please don't lie. As enticing as it is to take your significant other out to dinner on the company after you return from a business trip, don't do it. The $40 you will spend today is a drop in the bucket compared to the months of salary you'll lose if you're caught.

Now that you understand your company's policies, it's time to bid adieu to the Job Gods and get to work. In general, the less human resources is reminded of your existence, the better. Think of HR as a sleeping baby you don't want to disturb. Go about your business doing what you're supposed to do, but keep the noise level to a minimum.

On The Clock

During my first week at a financial consulting firm, I didn't have much work to do yet, so I decided to run out and catch up on the errands I'd missed while I was job hunting. I guess I ran over my lunch hour a few times, but I knew I'd be working 80 hours a week soon, so I didn't worry about it. Sure enough, within a few weeks, I was so busy I always ate lunch at my desk. So naturally, I was pretty surprised when my boss brought up attendance as an item of concern in my initial review. That first week, he'd seen me leaving the office a lot during business hours—but he hadn't paid attention to anything since then!

Kyra, 24, Ontario

One of my favorite managers used to say that perception is reality, and there is nothing stronger than a perception formed on the basis of a first impression. Whether you have a clock-watcher as a boss or not, it's crucial that you are on your best behavior during your first month at a new job. Be aware that everyone is watching you, so make sure to arrive on time for work. It's not a bad idea to be seen eating lunch at your desk a few times so that your coworkers keep that image in their minds. If you do go out, don't run over the allotted hour. At the end of the day, carefully watch what time people in your department leave the office. You should aim to depart at the midpoint. You don't want to be the first one out the door, but if you're the last one, you'll set a precedent that you are willing to work late for the rest of your days at that company. Also, because many employers think they are entitled to work twenty-something employees to death, make sure your boss and colleagues see early on that you have a life outside business hours.

In this age of instant accessibility, flexible workplaces, and virtual teams, it may seem ridiculous to be chained to your desk between the hours of 9 and 5 every Monday through Friday. However, the reality is that most of the corporate world is still pretty rigid about physical attendance. My friend Harry told me that his company's CEO stood at the window of his corner office and watched to see how many cars rolled through the gate one minute after 9 a.m. Remember that half the battle is showing up, so don't get caught by someone's attendance radar.

Additionally, while you're on the clock, stay busy doing the company's work. This might be challenging in the beginning because most managers have no clue what to do with new employees—it's either too late to involve you in an existing project, they do not trust you to handle anything that's on fire, or they do not have time to show you the ropes. Nevertheless, you don't have to sit at your desk twiddling your thumbs. Offer assistance to your managers and colleagues, and if anyone takes you up on the offer, make sure you do a better job than expected.

Inevitably, your days at a new job will involve administrative work in some shape or form. If you're a recent graduate, there is a good chance the company sold you on using your existing skills to do meaningful work. Therefore, you are probably insulted to be answering phones for the price of a college education. My best advice is to think of your time as an administrative assistant as a right of passage. Everyone must do it, and by the time you emerge from your mountain of executive expense reports, you will appreciate the mundane tasks that go into running a business, and you will also have the knowledge and experience to contribute in a consequential way. If you're a mid-level employee and someone requests that you assist with administrative work, do it with a smile. Yes, I realize that you paid your dues a long time ago, but that person might not know you blistered your fingers making 7 million photocopies as an admin. Trust me, you won't be doing it forever. Provided you command a higher salary than an admin, the company will want to leverage your skills elsewhere.

When your manager involves you in a project that includes coworkers, resist the temptation to jump in and take over. Do more than your share of listening and ask for direction from your teammates rather than suggesting your own course of action. Nothing turns people off like a newbie who waltzes in and says, "Well, at my old company, we did it like this." The second that this comes out of your mouth, people will think that if things were so swell at your old company, maybe you should go back. This is the last thing you want. For the sake of your corporate persona, use your first projects as an opportunity to observe how things are done at your new company. You'll have your time in the sun soon enough.

During your first weeks, use any free time to research your position and brainstorm project concepts. Reading is fine too, but keep the content to industry publications, human resources material, or anything related to the company or your job. Show your boss what you've learned by sharing ideas, highlighting key points in printed articles, and asking questions. She will think that you are hungry and prepared to hit the ground running, which, my friend, is exactly how stellar reputations are made.

21 Tips for Road Warriors

Your new position may require business travel, and the first time your boss tells you that you're shipping out of town, you'll probably jump for joy. After all, this is exciting stuff. Not only will you be escaping the office, but you'll also be spending your company's dime to sleep in a king-size bed by yourself and sample cuisine from a new city's finest restaurants. And don't forget about those free mini-shampoos in the hotel!

After awhile, the magic of business travel wears off. You find that your trips away from the office involve working more hours, not less. You return, exhausted, with a bag full of dry cleaning and a week's worth of e-mails to catch up on. But for better or for worse, business travel is a part of life for many corporate employees. Here are a few tips to make your trips more bearable:

1. **Understand your company's expense rules.** Look out! Corporate expense policies are riddled with fine print. Some companies won't allow you to take a taxi to the airport. Others won't pay for your lunch because you'd be buying it yourself if you were in the office.

2. **Keep a bag packed at home.** You never know when you're going to need to travel out of town on short notice. Prevent frazzled, last-minute rushing around by keeping a travel bag packed and ready to go in your closet. Besides a suit and comfortable business shoes, include toiletries, regular medications, mints, business cards, and modem and power cords for your laptop.

3. **Remember your corporate persona.** Out of the office does not mean off the job. Resist the urge to let your hair down and party during a business trip. There's nothing wrong with having fun, but you should behave

professionally, no matter whom you're with or what you're doing. You never know who's watching.

4. **Review your itinerary ahead of time.** Go over your schedule to make sure you know where you're supposed to be at all times and how you're going to get there. Leave large time cushions in between each activity so that you can make it from one place to the next without having a heart attack.

5. **Sign up for a frequent flyer account.** Frequent flyer miles are the best way to make your business travel hassles pay off. My husband and I went to Australia on miles we earned traveling for our respective jobs. While you're at it, make sure the credit card you use for business is linked to a frequent flyer program too.

6. **Print out important materials.** You never know when your laptop is going to decide to have a temper tantrum. Technology often fails us on business trips, so if you really need something for a meeting, carry both hard and virtual copies.

7. **Assign colleagues to share your workload.** Keep the machine running by making a detailed list of tasks you need covered while you're gone and delegating each one to a trusted colleague. Set up your e-mail and voice mail systems with an "Out of the Office" message, complete with emergency contact information.

8. **Pack necessities in your carry-on bag.** Once your Samsonite disappears down the conveyor belt and into that black hole, you can't control where it ends up. Of course, 99 percent of the time, your baggage will make it safely to your destination. Even so, have a contingency plan, just in case.

9. **Block out the noise.** A good night's sleep is imperative to your effectiveness on a business trip. Regardless of where you're going, assume that your hotel will be

louder than a big city apartment building, and pack earplugs or a travel-size white noise machine, such as those from Sharper Image or HoMedics.

10. **Carry snacks and a bottle of water.** In the alternate universe known as business travel, something as simple as eating can turn into a complex task you can't be bothered with. In case you have to miss a meal, tide yourself over with a granola bar or a health bar. And don't forget to stay hydrated, especially when you're flying.

11. **Dress up, not down.** When you're attending meetings in unfamiliar surroundings, wear business-appropriate attire. Even if the folks you're meeting with are dressed casually, no one will fault you for being the only one in a suit. Pack your clothes in a garment bag and use the iron in your hotel room to keep your attire looking neat and wrinkle-free.

12. **Roll your laptop.** Save yourself an excruciating backache by rolling a laptop carry case instead of lugging it around on your shoulder. You'd be surprised how heavy all of that computer hardware can be after a day on the road.

13. **Fly during business hours.** Inevitably, taking a business trip means working longer hours anyway, so don't be a martyr and volunteer to take a red-eye flight. You're already stressed, so why should you be bone-tired too? Also, don't feel obligated to work during the flight out. Use the time to relax and mentally prepare yourself for the trip ahead.

14. **Pay someone to drive you around.** Even if you take pride in your sense of direction, do you really want to be bothered with navigating a rental car through the bowels of a strange city? If your company will allow it, stick to taxis or corporate cars. Just don't forget to carry extra money! You will need to pay your driver in

cash, so multiple or long trips will often cost more money than you may typically carry in your wallet.

15. **Call the office frequently.** Never allow your boss to think you've dropped off the face of the earth—even if you're super busy. Drop her a voice mail or an e-mail to update her on your whereabouts, and don't let her catch you spending half a day gambling in the Las Vegas airport.

16. **Log on at the hotel.** Connect to the Internet in your room using your modem, or make an evening pilgrimage to your hotel's business center. Try to check your e-mail at least once a day so that you can keep on top of the endless stream of issues and action items back at the office. Even if your boss isn't expecting you to do this, you'll be grateful you did after you return to work when your trip is over. Just watch the hotel's fees!

17. **Check your watch and wake-up calls.** When you arrive in a new time zone, reset your watch and the time on your cell phone immediately in order to avoid confusion later on. Also, don't rely on your alarm clock or the hotel's wake-up call alone to make sure you're on time for a morning meeting. Use both, just in case.

18. **Don't touch the hotel phone.** Use your cell phone or a calling card. Calls from a hotel phone, even local ones, may be so pricey you should be embarrassed to expense them. Even if you're not embarrassed, your company's expense department is probably too smart to pay for them.

19. **Take advantage of the hotel's fitness center.** Running on the treadmill or lifting weights is a great way to relieve stress and to work off those extra pounds you've put on from eating out every day.

20. **Have dinner with friends or family instead of your co-workers.** Does anyone from your personal life live in

the city where you're traveling? Make an effort to get together instead of hanging out with the same colleagues you see all day. Business travel is a great way to catch up with folks you wouldn't get to spend time with otherwise.

21. **Extend your stay to do some sightseeing.** If your company is paying for you to fly to a city you've never visited, why not stay the weekend and treat yourself to some fun activities? There's nothing more frustrating than being in New York City from Monday through Thursday and spending the entire time in a convention center.

I've logged more than 100 business trips, and I still get tripped up by some of these. Just the other day, I arrived at JFK Airport only to find that my flight to Washington was departing from La Guardia. If only I had reviewed my itinerary ahead of time! Learn how to travel smart, however, and your experiences as a road warrior can add a rewarding new dimension to your job.

Chapter 2 Take Home Points

✓ **Combat stereotypes.** Prepare for the challenge of being stereotyped according to your age. Paying close attention to your appearance and how you introduce yourself to new colleagues will ensure that you come across as a mature professional.

✓ **Take your work seriously.** At the start of a new job, no conversation or assignment should be taken lightly. Opinions formed from initial interactions are very difficult to change.

✓ **Observe your new company's culture.** Adapt your behavior and work style to fit within your company's boundaries. The most successful employees are those who assimilate quickly.

✓ **Remember that perception is reality.** Be on your best behavior during the first few weeks at a new job.

Chapter 3

Working the Crowd

Now that you have the big-picture view of your new company, it is time to get to know people one-on-one. Establishing strong on-the-job relationships will drive your career growth and give you a reason to come to work in the morning. When you first meet new colleagues, it's hard to imagine having an informal lunch meeting with them or talking reality television in front of the watercooler. You might think that your fellow employees should approach you because *you* are the new kid. However, in most companies, the pace of business is so frenetic that you'll be lucky if people even notice you've arrived to work in the morning. It's your responsibility to make sure that you are professionally and socially integrated into your department, and you'll be better off if you take action sooner rather than later. In this chapter, I'll discuss strategies for getting to know your new boss and navigating your company's social scene. I'll also touch on how to practice cringe-free networking and how to scout out the antidote for corporate insanity—your mentor.

Getting to Know the Boss

My immediate supervisor was so disorganized that it drove me up the wall. He was so busy trying to find his way out from underneath his desk that he was unable to communicate any vision whatsoever. His style put me off so much that I started to get really bitter. Eventually I could see my attitude seeping into our interactions, and I think my boss could tell that I didn't like him. Soon he found subtle ways to let me know he felt the same way, and the next thing I knew, I was getting all of the most boring assignments. I didn't want to sabotage my career, so I tried focusing on my boss's strengths. I found that he was a great listener and that he could talk sports with greater finesse than my husband. By making a conscious effort to value what he brought to the table, I was able to turn things around between us.

Dvora, 26, Florida

There are as many different types of bosses in the corporate world as there are people, and, hopefully, the manager you've chosen is a good fit for you. As the captain of your department's ship, your boss is responsible for the group's success and, to a great extent, your own. As such, it's crucial that you get to know your immediate supervisor early and determine her priorities. During your first days in the trenches, observe your boss in action. If you can, shadow her for a day to see how she interacts with junior and senior employees, and how she handles different situations. Business consultant C. Sam Benson, in his article "Your Management Success," defines the following basic management styles:

- *Aggressive*: competitive, decisive, direct, likes immediate results.
- *Persuasive*: poised, optimistic, convincing, likes interacting with people.
- *Supportive*: patient, reliable, a good listener, likes security.
- *Analytical*: precise, prepared, plans thoroughly, dislikes mistakes.

It's difficult to slap a label on a complex person you barely know, but thinking about your boss's management style will help you determine how to proceed with the best chance of success. You may have heard that there are documented variations between male and female bosses. Supposedly, women are more nurturing, collaborative, and relationship-focused, but they may react emotionally when they feel threatened or insecure. On the other hand, men are presumed to be more generous and easygoing, but they tend to favor individual work on tasks and an autocratic approach to decision-making. I haven't noticed such clear-cut differences, and I don't know that you will either. As you get to know your boss, I urge you not to put much stock in stereotypes. Now that a female manager is no longer an anomaly, I think you'll find that the way your boss operates will depend almost exclusively on her unique personality, and that gender will play little, if any, role.

It's a good idea to set up a one-on-one meeting with your new boss right away. You will need to be proactive about this because, in the crazed atmosphere of the corporate world, your boss may be too harried to make the suggestion. If necessary, block an hour with his admin or ask him to grab a quick lunch in the cafeteria. New York City career counselor Judith Gerberg suggests three strategies for this first encounter: 1) express gratitude and enthusiasm, 2) clarify roles and expectations, and 3) define the training and support you will need to do your job well. Additionally, you'll want to leave the meeting with answers to the following questions:

- What are your daily responsibilities?
- Are there department meetings he would like you to be a part of? Are there particular people he would suggest you meet?
- What is the best way to get in touch with him if you need something (for instance, does he want you to drop by his office, would he prefer a voice mail, or is e-mail best)?
- How should you document your work? How often and in what format does he want you to report on project status?
- How should you go about suggesting new ideas or processes?
- How will your performance be evaluated?

If you can accomplish one thing in this initial meeting, make sure you and your boss agree on how to move forward. All of your efforts to impress him with your expansive knowledge of the field and your creative ideas will be fruitless if the two of you are going in different directions. Find out what he wants from you first, and then brainstorm ways to surpass his expectations. You can also establish a good rapport by making your new boss feel needed. Show him in the very beginning that you are ready and willing to be guided, and bond with him over the fact that he has some years on you, and, therefore, has a treasure trove of career advice to offer.

How else can you get started on the right foot? Here are some other hints:

1. **Be humble.** Don't approach your boss with a sense of entitlement, as though he is personally responsible for furthering your career. Instead, focus on learning what you can do to make his life easier, contribute to your company's goals, and make him look good to *his* boss.

2. **Be realistic.** Keep in mind that your boss is a human being and that he is going to make mistakes. He is not *trying* to make your life difficult. The two of you are on the same team, so don't be overly sensitive or critical. Listen without judgment, make a sincere effort to understand your boss's position, and patiently explain your ideas. If you're unclear about something, ask for clarification rather than expecting him to read your mind.

3. **Be honest.** Admit if you do something wrong, and then ask your boss how you can rectify the situation. Don't allow yourself to get caught in a maze of lies or excuses that will result in a loss of credibility.

4. **Be respectful of your boss's time.** Appear in his office with a checklist of things you need to cover, and don't dwell too long on any particular subject. Your boss will be more receptive to meeting with you if he knows you'll be in and out of his office quickly.

5. **Be self-sufficient.** Only approach your boss with a problem or complaint if you've explored all options for resolving it yourself. When you

do, be prepared to have a solution at hand that you could implement with his help. Choose your battles wisely, and decide carefully if bringing an issue to your boss's attention is really necessary or if you would be better off letting it go.

6. **Be friendly.** Encourage your boss to genuinely like you. If he expresses an outrageous political opinion or offers unsolicited advice about your personal life, nod and smile. You don't have to agree, but you don't have to disagree either. Your boss's feelings should be protected at all times. Compliment him on his tie or presentation, if it's appropriate, and thank him profusely for any efforts on your behalf. Do personal favors for him and brownnose all you want, but make sure you do it sincerely. Your boss will smell phoniness a million miles away—and believe me, he won't appreciate it. Even if your boss isn't someone you'd choose as a friend, focus on the things about him you do like, and do your best to establish a positive working relationship.

7. **Be a "can-do" employee.** When your boss asks you to do something, accommodate him, if possible. The words *I don't have time* should never escape your lips. If you know something needs to be done, do it without being prodded, and if your boss asks for help in a group setting, be the first to volunteer. Your boss will quickly come to see you as a huge asset to the team and as someone he can count on.

An important caveat to the "can-do" mantra: You have to set reasonable boundaries for your new manager. There is a fine line between being a hard worker and letting people take advantage of you. Some managers, even good ones, fall victim to the *gofer syndrome*. If you've ever made a photocopy for a boss who has a Xerox machine in his office, you know what I'm talking about. The gofer syndrome involves a stream of barked orders to the tune of, "Do this, do that, get me this, get me that, tell this person ABC, and get an answer from that person on XYZ." Pretty soon, you're spending so much time on silly errands that you don't have time to get any real work done. Cure your boss of the gofer syndrome by telling him that you're happy to make those copies if he will give you permission to de-prioritize the report you're working on for the CEO. Your boss will see for himself how he should best utilize your time.

Also, don't let your boss catch you staying until 10 p.m. or obsessively checking e-mail on weekends unless you want her to expect that behavior from you for the duration of your career. Along those same lines, you shouldn't impose a performance standard on yourself that is impossible to maintain. If you return all of your boss's e-mails or voice mails within 5 minutes of receiving them and complete assignments way ahead of deadlines, you run the risk of disappointing her when you can't deliver.

One more piece of advice: Get to know coworkers who report to the same manager quickly so that you can probe them about your boss's pet peeves, preferences, and expectations. Be careful how you phrase your questions, though, because you don't want to launch a discussion that criticizes your new boss in any way. Ask a colleague to fill you in on the chain of command in your department. Use this information to introduce yourself and explain your function in the office to your boss's boss and the other managers you'll be working with. Establishing strong relationships with the department higher-ups will accomplish the dual functions of making your boss look good and strengthening your overall position in the company.

The Corporate Social Scene

When I moved to San Francisco to start a new marketing job in the cosmetics industry, I really wanted to make friends with the younger people in my department. I tried to get to know the girls who worked in the cubes around me, but they were such a tight-knit group that I thought I was back in high school. Every time I'd ask one of them to go to lunch, she would come up with some excuse, and then later I would see her leaving with one of our other colleagues. Then one day, I saw the girl next to me thumbing through a bridal magazine. I walked up to her and asked her about her wedding. She was more than happy to talk about it, and when I told her I was from St. Louis (where she was getting married), she couldn't stop asking me questions.

Preeti, 24, California

Imagine being stranded on a desert island with your coworkers. Scary, huh? But when you think about it, you spend just as much time with them at work as you would if you were all breaking coconuts over your knees in the South Pacific. Therefore, if you want to enjoy your job, it's in your best interest to make friends with some of these folks. Work friends will be there when you want to grab a bite at the restaurant down the block or take a quick turn on the treadmill at the gym. They'll be there when you need to commiserate about a project or vent about a new company policy. They may even be around when your world changes forever, such as when my colleagues and I watched the September 11 terrorist attack on the World Trade Center. Work friendships make the corporate world bearable, and you shouldn't try to make do without them.

The ideal time to scout out potential work friendships is at the start of a new job. When your boss introduces you to the other members of your team, make a note of people your age who look friendly. Take them up on their offers to help you. Maybe you already know how to order business cards, but there's no harm in finding an excuse to talk to your new coworkers. If someone asks you to get a cup of coffee, go gladly, but don't jump at the chance for a friend so quickly that you end up spending all of your time with one particular person. Because you're unfamiliar with people's allegiances, you need to avoid aligning yourself with a single colleague or group of colleagues. In your first month, you should aim to know a little about a lot of people rather than the other way around.

Once you're established in the department, make an effort to get to know potential work friends personally. This can be intimidating and even somewhat difficult if your office is full of cliques. It's possible that a group of your coworkers will go out to happy hour and leave you sitting at your desk feeling like the new kid in 3rd grade all over again. The only way to break through work social groups is by one person at a time. Zero in on the most approachable person in the group, find out what interests him, and then weave these things into a conversation. For example, if you see that your next-door neighbor has a Nerf basketball net in his cube, you might ask him if he caught the Final Four game last night. People love to talk about themselves, so encourage potential friends to tell you about their lives. Listen to what they say, and talk about yourself only if asked. Doing someone a favor is also a good friend-making strategy. Suppose one of your teammates is frantically looking for a last-minute pet sitter while she goes out of town on business. If you live in her neighborhood, graciously offer to feed her cats. Your teammate won't forget this act of goodwill, and will be likely to view you favorably in the future.

Sometimes team members will be nonresponsive to your gestures of friendship. Don't take it personally. Your department's culture might encourage people to keep to themselves, or you and your coworkers might not have much in common. If this is the case, expand your search to the rest of the company. Perhaps you should get to know the girl from accounting a little better. What about that guy who always rides the elevator with you in the morning?

In addition, check with human resources to see if your company sponsors out-of-office activities, such as sports teams, travel clubs, or charity initiatives. Sign up for "extracurriculars" that catch your eye and commit to attend events. Once you're there, find someone you know, and ask him to introduce you around. Remember, like everything in the corporate world, new work friendships require follow-up. When you meet someone interesting, think of an excuse to drop him an e-mail afterwards. You'll remind him who you are and encourage him to make contact again.

A word on dating in the corporate world: Don't go out with someone in your company unless you can handle seeing that person every day if the relationship doesn't work out. Definitely avoid dating your boss or anyone on your immediate team. Even if you end up marrying that person, it won't be worth the career complications. The best idea? Get your colleagues to introduce you to their single friends!

Work Friends vs. Real Friends

I will never forget it. I was standing on the corner of 43rd Street and Broadway in New York City with my co-worker Laura. Laura and I had been through a lot together in the year we had worked on the same public relations account team. We had coped with ego-obsessed executives and unreasonable clients, and we had implemented innovative and creative ideas neither of us knew we had in us. Nearly every day, Laura and I had lunch together to dish about our projects and the latest goings-on in our personal lives.

Standing on the corner, I said to Laura, "I'm so glad you're one of my closest friends."

She looked at me strangely. "Alex," she said. "There's a difference between close friends and people you talk to at work. You know that, right?"

Laura's response may have been a little harsh, but it taught me an important lesson about work friends vs. real friends: It's easy to mistake one for the other, especially when you're struggling to establish a social life. In school, making friends is as simple as walking over to the dorm room next door and plopping down on the bed. After college, however, there are no such opportunities. Because you might be too busy to go out and meet new people, the tendency is to target your coworkers. It makes sense. After all, they might be the only people you know that are your age, and you see them for 8 hours every day.

While many people use work as a springboard for building strong friendships outside the office, I wouldn't assume your colleagues are your new best friends just because you take your coffee breaks together. Laura was right—there are differences between close friends who will be there for you through life's tough times and people you hang out with while you happen to be stuck in the same building. You can spare yourself disappointment later on by noting the differences between a work friend and a real friend. Here are some questions to ask yourself:

- If your friend left the company, would you still be in touch with her in a year?
- If you had a personal emergency, would you consider asking your friend for help?
- Do you hang out with your friend outside the office? (Weekday lunch, happy hour, and business trips don't count.)
- Have you met your friend's significant other? What about her friends outside the office?
- If your friend received the promotion you were banking on, would you be genuinely happy for her?
- If you ran into your friend in the grocery store, would you be able to talk to her for 10 minutes without mentioning work?
- Do you have your friend's personal e-mail address?
- Have you seen where your friend lives?
- Do you and your friend have anything in common besides your age and your job?

If you answered yes to most of these questions, you might have found yourself a real friend at work. Take care of this relationship by making a concerted effort to spend time with your friend outside the office. You and your friend should also avoid working together too closely. Like living with close friends, being in business with them can sometimes be disastrous. Whether we like it or not, people can behave differently when money, power, and careers are at stake. Suppose you and your friend pair up for a high-profile, new business project. Your friend could be the kindest, most generous person in the world after quitting time, but she might take all the credit and do none of the work in the office. You don't want to put yourself in a situation where you must choose between your friendship and your career.

If you're lucky, someone you meet at work could turn into a friend for life. It happened to me. My friend Kathryn and I started our PR careers in the same department six years ago, and she was the maid of honor in my wedding!

On the Outside

A few years ago, I was working for a dot-com. My coworkers smoked pot a lot, and I knew they thought I had a pole up the you-know-what for always turning them down. I really wanted to get along with them, so one night while we were away at a conference, I got high with them in a hotel room. I thought there was no way our boss would find out, but somehow she did. She told me she expected more of me as a senior manager. I was lucky I didn't get fired.

Kim, 29, Washington

Happy hour, team lunches, holiday parties, you name it—there are plenty of opportunities to socialize in the corporate world. Partaking in these outings gets you out of sterile "Cube City" and allows you to pretend you actually have a life. The thought of free food alone is enough to put you in a good mood. So by all means, go to these events and have a blast. Just keep a couple of things in the back of your mind.

It's tempting to let loose with your colleagues, especially when you're out of the office. However, you should never let alcohol (or drugs) get the best of you. Remember how your college roommate said you were the biggest blabbermouth on campus after you'd had a few? Just think of what you might have to say about your job, your boss, and your coworkers if you get smashed with them. When your boss waves his corporate credit card, it's easy to get caught up in the excitement of free rounds on the company, so you should prepare for this situation in advance.

A few hours before you go out to the restaurant or bar, eat a hefty meal and drink plenty of water. Once you're there, do not get drunk. It's tough enough to maintain your corporate persona when you're perfectly sober, but when alcohol steals your inhibition, you might find yourself saying and doing things you'd ordinarily consider big no-no's. I'm not going to say you can't consume alcohol, because we're all adults. In fact, if you repeatedly shun drinking in your colleagues' company, you might be perceived as weird or a loser. The key is to find the middle ground. No matter how much peer pressure comes your way, you should stick to one drink (two if you have a high tolerance). Pretend it's Pepto-Bismol, sip it super slow, and it will last the whole evening. Take heart—you can still party with the best of them, just save it for your best friend's tapas party or your Friday night poker game.

The good news is that drinking is not typically the focus when the boss takes the team out for lunch. The bad news is that you have to watch more closely what you say and do, because people are actually paying attention. When the group arrives at the restaurant, don't sit next to your manager at the big table. You'll look like a brownnoser to your coworkers. Plus, if conversations split off, guess who you'll be stuck talking to? Also, don't be the first one to order. Note whether your colleagues are ordering drinks and the price of their entrées, and then follow suit with a selection that is perfectly in line with what everyone else is having. And roll your eyes if you must, but I have to put it out there: Watch the table manners. Remember the dating rules your mother told you when you were getting dressed for your prom? Avoid talking while you're chewing, and don't order anything you have to eat with your hands or is a stain waiting to happen. If the table is sharing dishes, don't hog. Eating out with the team is different than eating out with your friends. Relax, tell jokes, have fun—but don't forget that business is business, and you're still on the clock.

And finally, there comes a time each year when the corporate world becomes a symbol of cheesy sentiment and material excess. Yes, it's the holiday season. And while your coworkers are turning your floor into a red and green monstrosity, and the mailroom guys are lugging a 10-foot-tall menorah into the lobby, you are probably deciding whether to go to the company's annual holiday party. For the sake of your career, you should make an appearance. And because your company is going to spend your raise on a dancing Christmas tree whether you enjoy it or not, you might as well make the best of the situation. Mind your corporate persona, and dress appropriately for the occasion. If you're allowed to bring a date, treat someone you love (or someone you owe a favor) to a catered meal. If not, use the opportunity to get some face time with higher-ups you wouldn't get to meet otherwise.

Your department might also have its own party. Relax—these are fun! Spare yourself stress by finding out in advance about the company policy on giving gifts. Hopefully, your department favors the *grab bag*—a convention in which each person in the group puts one small wrapped gift in the pool, and then leaves with someone else's even smaller wrapped gift. If you're supposed to shop for your entire group, however, keep your gifts thoughtful albeit slightly impersonal. You're not required to give your boss anything, but it is a nice gesture. You should always buy the group admin something as a token of your appreciation for all of her help during the year. Departmental holiday parties often have a potluck component as well. Don't panic while your coworkers are competing to see who can cook the best holiday fare. Go to the grocery store and buy a $2 package of Duncan Hines chocolate chip cookie mix, spend 10 minutes baking the stuff, and pass the goodies off as homemade at the party. I guarantee your colleagues will say your cookies are the best they've ever tasted.

Conversation Taboos

When we're in our 20s, the tendency is to believe that the world revolves around us. In the corporate world, this attitude can lead to paranoia. Suddenly, you're afraid to talk to anyone lest he stab you in the back or underhandedly steal your promotion. Understand, though, that your colleagues are too busy with their own agendas most of the time to worry about getting you in trouble. So instead of staying up all night worrying whether or not your cagey workmate is going to spread rumors about you, follow these simple work conversation rules and rest easy:

1. **Don't spread gossip.** This one is first because it's the toughest to avoid. Dishing the dirt at work is fun, especially if you're bored. Listen all you want, but refrain from contributing to conversations that could compromise

someone's reputation. Damaging stories spread like a conflagration, and being nailed as the source can be a career killer.

2. **Don't swear.** Nothing taints your corporate persona as much as foul language. There are people all over the business world who spew curse words, and maybe your boss is one of them. If you're tempted to join in, remember where the phrase "potty mouth" came from. In the corporate world, you don't want to look or smell like you were anywhere near the potty, so don't sound like it either.

3. **Don't be politically incorrect.** Just because we all crack up when Saturday Night Live makes fun of PC in the workplace doesn't mean we shouldn't take it seriously on Monday morning. Realize that people are ultrasensitive about issues of political correctness and that, as far as work is concerned, you should have no opinions. If you've noticed certain stereotypes to be true, keep your observations to yourself, and make sure to steer clear of racist or sexist jokes.

4. **Don't talk about sex, drugs, or politics.** I don't care how liberal your office is or how convinced you are that your colleagues will understand your point of view, if you wouldn't discuss it with your grandmother or your religious leader, mum's the word in the corporate world.

5. **Don't share secrets.** Really need to keep a secret? Don't tell anyone. If you need to preface a statement with "promise you won't tell a soul" or "don't tell anyone I said this," you shouldn't be saying it. The only people you

can trust with secrets at work are the folks who fall into the "real friend" category we talked about earlier, and even then you should be wary. Think about it: Would you trust each friend in your close-knit college clan with a secret that could ruin your reputation if it got out? Exactly. If you absolutely must tell someone you're looking for a new job, for example, call your mom.

Working Your Net

I still can't stomach the whole networking thing. I was recently at a conference where I saw a guy who graduated from my school a few years ahead of me. I'd read something about him in the alumni magazine. He had an amazing job in my field, and I wanted to go talk to him more than anything. In the end, though, I was too self-conscious. Why on earth would this guy want to help me, and what right did I have to ask him anyway? I didn't want to feel like a slimy car salesman, so I left. I knew I probably blew a great opportunity, but I just couldn't make myself do it.

Manuel, 25, Colorado

A popular misconception among twenty-somethings is that networking is about getting a job. In reality, it's much more than that. Michael Alexander of FindAMentor (*www.findamentor.org*) defines *networking* as "working a net to catch information." It's about establishing relationships that provide you with valuable feedback and allow you to make educated decisions. You do it every day without even realizing it. Let's look at an example: Suppose within days of your move to a new town, your car breaks down. How would you handle this situation? Would you open the yellow pages and take your car to the first mechanic you see, or would you ask your colleagues for a recommendation? The second option is an example of networking. Think about why many successful businesses don't need to advertise. They obtain new clients by word of mouth—otherwise known as networking!

The purpose of business networking is to gain information, increase your visibility in your field, and establish personal connections that will help you move forward in your career. Even if you're happy with your job, you should always be looking ahead to the next one. How do you use networking as a tool to prepare for your career's future? There are a few steps involved in this process:

✓ **Step One:** Look for ways to expand your business networks. Judith Gerberg, career counselor and director of Gerberg & Co. in New York City, recommends looking beyond your company for business contacts so that your networking will have lifelong continuity, regardless of the specific jobs you hold. She suggests joining professional organizations that you have a genuine interest in and attending at least one activity a month. At the same time, you should habitually ask people in your circle if they know anyone who might be a good contact for you. At its core, networking should be fun. If you seek out people who care about the same things you do, you'll enjoy networking and won't view it as a chore.

✓ **Step Two:** Know what you want from your contacts and what *you* can offer *them*. Many people dislike networking because they think that asking a stranger for help is an imposition. Remember that it's human nature to want to help someone, and I think you'll find that most people will be receptive, provided you approach them the right way. If you know you're going to be meeting potential contacts, don't just drop a pile of business cards in your briefcase and call it a day. Prepare for networking conversations in advance by considering what you need from the contact. Will a phone conversation do, or would you like to meet your contact for coffee or a meal? Additionally, Rachel Solar-Tuttle, coauthor of *Table Talk*, says that because networking is collaboration, every time you ask for something or meet with a potential contact, you should think about how you can help him in return. Listen to your contacts carefully so that you can glean insights about how you might assist them. Remember that networking is like karma—what goes around comes around.

✓ **Step Three:** Contact the person. When approaching a potential contact, be friendly, respectful, and brief. In Chapter 1, we talked about how e-mail usually achieves better results than a phone call, but if you are attending a networking event, an in-person conversation is often the best option of all. No matter how you make contact, always keep in mind that the person is doing you a favor. If he's in the middle of something, don't interrupt, and be conscious of his time commitments. When you sit down with your contact one-on-one, offer to pay any expenses associated with the meeting, and remember to send him a thank-you note afterward.

✓ **Step Four:** Follow up with your contact regularly. After a successful first networking meeting, it's your responsibility to keep the lines of communication open. Did your contact give you any advice or suggest a course of action? If so, touch base every so often to remind him who you are and to keep him apprised of your progress. Be aware of his career moves, and make sure he stays informed of yours. Invite him to get together again, and, during the holiday season, send him a card with a nice note.

Even the most natural networking interactions can be challenging if you're shy. You might not like asking people for anything, whether it's advice about a particular industry or a piece of gum. I overcome my anxiety by talking to potential contacts about the aspects of my career I feel most strongly about. Should a networking opportunity present itself during an impromptu conversation, I make a conscious effort to be myself and stick to subjects I know well. When making a networking call, I jot down a few notes so that I won't forget what I want to say. I schedule time for these in the morning when my energy level is high. I also make it a point to stand up during each call, because I tend to sound more professional when I do so. After several years of practice, I'm still nervous talking to people I don't know. However, every time I do it and experience a positive outcome, I gain a little more confidence. I promise that you will too!

Recruiting a Mentor

You may have heard that the best way to advance in your career is to find a good mentor. A *mentor* is a person, usually older, who can advise you on matters relevant to your career, and who offers support and direction as you progress in your field. Obviously, having a mentor is a good idea, but he won't come to you. You have to seek him out and proactively establish the relationship. Doing this is easier said than done, because the best mentors are typically not your direct supervisors, and you may need to look outside your immediate department. Organizational psychologist Neil Stroul recommends that you observe powerful individuals in your company and approach someone who possesses a "generosity of spirit"—or a natural willingness to go out of his way to help others. Ideally, this person will have already passed through the part of the career path that you are currently on, and will have achieved success by making smart decisions and learning from his experiences. He will be someone you like and admire, and someone whose values you share.

Once you target a potential mentor, how do you ask for his help? First of all, treat your mentor-to-be as you would any other networking contact by preparing in advance. You should determine what you are looking for and devise a tentative schedule for how often you would like to meet. Make sure your expectations are reasonable, because the potential mentor is unlikely to agree if he thinks he will have to meet with you every week or act as a referee between you and your boss. When contacting the person, briefly explain why you are seeking his guidance. Compliment him sincerely, and ask if he would be amenable to an in-person meeting. Upon sitting down face to face, reiterate your thanks, and lay out your vision for the relationship. Read the person's reaction. Hopefully, he will be as enthusiastic as you are, and the two of you can set up a timeline for future meetings. But if he isn't, now is the time to find out. You don't want a mentor who is meeting with you out of a sense of obligation.

Michael Alexander of FindAMentor offers some tips for making the most of a mentor relationship:

- Ask lots of questions.
- Practice listening.
- Answer questions truthfully. (When the truth is withheld—even a little—the information provided by your mentor may not be accurate.)
- Filter information consciously before accepting it as true and right for you.
- Understand your mentor's desire to help, and take feedback you don't like in stride.
- Respect your mentor's time constraints and other commitments.

Don't forget to show your mentor the appreciation he deserves for giving you the benefit of his experience. Follow up on your commitments to him, and brainstorm ways to help him in return. For example, one of my early mentors was a senior vice president at my PR firm. One of her favorite hobbies is yoga, so when she wanted to write an article about it for a healthy living magazine, I volunteered to edit it. Also, consider helping someone else. What's the best thing you can do when you've been fortunate enough to find a good mentor? Become one yourself! By sharing your wisdom and expertise with someone less experienced, you can give back some of the goodwill your mentor showed to you.

Chapter 3 Take Home Points

✓ **Get to know your immediate supervisor early.** Determine her priorities, find out what she wants from you, and brainstorm ways to surpass her expectations.

✓ **Master the corporate social scene.** In your first month, aim to know a little about a lot of people rather than the other way around. Once you're established in the department, make personal connections with potential work friends.

✓ **Understand the different types of friendships.** Know that there are differences between close friends, who will be there for you through life's tough times, and work friends, who you hang out with while you're stuck in the same building. Adjust your expectations accordingly.

✓ **Expand your business networks.** Business networking is a valuable tool to gain information, increase your visibility in your field, and establish relationships that will help you move forward in your career. Seek out new contacts and potential mentors whom you like and admire, as well as those whose interests you share.

Chapter 4

Be the Master
of Your Plan

At 22, I had been an overachiever all my life. So naturally, I expected to experience success beyond my wildest dreams at my first company. I was going to go in there and kick the corporate world's ass. As soon as they saw what I was made of, I was sure they'd make me the company's youngest vice president. I put so much pressure on myself to know everything right away that I nearly collapsed under the weight of my own unrealistic expectations.

Your first jobs are not meant to be the be-all and end-all of career stardom. How can you master the skills it takes to get ahead without putting in any time in the trenches? That's like saying you could win an Olympic gold medal in swimming without learning to doggie paddle first. Look at your first post-college positions as temporary stops on your career path instead of as permanent ones. You are getting paid to learn everything you can so that snagging the next job isn't quite as challenging. This chapter will describe how to make the most out of your first job, knowing that you probably won't stay there forever. I'll start by sharing how you can set goals that further your personal mission. Next, I'll discuss strategies for adding value to your company and for developing critical career skills such as risk-taking and problem-solving, which will be useful no matter where you go or what you do. As you're reading, imagine your current company as a training ground to practice everything I cover.

Setting and Achieving Goals

> My first job at a nonprofit organization was nothing like I thought it would be. My responsibilities didn't remotely resemble what we discussed in the interview. I was eager to be out in the field helping people. Instead, I was stuck behind a desk pushing paper every day. I was really depressed until I asked myself, 'What can I take away from this that will help me get where I want to go?' When I took a step back, I realized that I first had to understand the mechanics of how a nonprofit works—and I wouldn't be able to learn that out in the field. I had to spend time doing exactly what I was doing.
>
> Tamika, 24, Washington, D.C.

Let's be realistic. Most junior-level jobs in the corporate world have a low glamour factor. As I talked about briefly in Chapter 2, twenty-somethings are required to pay their dues regardless of their education, and there's a good chance your responsibilities have nothing to do with what the interviewer promised. I'm willing to bet that they're more administrative, less creative, and less empowering.

This situation can be frustrating, especially if you're used to accomplishing a lot in a short period of time. You'll be much happier, though, if you look at your time on the bottom rung as an opportunity, instead of lamenting the tragic turn your once promising life has taken. Keep in mind what's really important to you and use this situation to acquire valuable skills and experience that will take you there. The easiest way to do this is to set specific, reasonable, and attainable goals for your present position that correspond to your long-term career strategy.

In his book *Getting Promoted: Real Strategies for Advancing Your Career*, Harry Chambers defines *goal-setting* as a positive statement that proclaims your expectations of growth and achievement. You want your goals to motivate you rather than discourage you, so they shouldn't be too ambitious. Instead, make them just tough enough so that you'll stay involved, constantly putting forth effort and reaching for that brass ring. Devise meaningful career goals by considering the following:

- *What* you're going to do.
- *Why* you want to do it and *how* it furthers your personal agenda.
- *When* you're going to do it.
- *How* you'll know when you've done it, and *how* you'll measure your success.

For example, a few years ago, I set the following goal for leveraging my present job responsibilities to further my big-picture agenda:

- **Current Role:** Work with teleconferencing company to coordinate weekly conference calls between the New York and UK offices.
- **Big-Picture Agenda:** Serve as the lead on a global PR account team.

- **Goal:** Master protocol for conducting global account team status calls.
  - *What I'm going to do*: In addition to setting up the calls, ask the VP for permission to listen and take notes.
  - *Why I want to do it*: By observing how global team account management is done, I will be better equipped to do it myself in the future.
  - *When I'm going to do it*: Talk to the VP on Monday and arrange to participate in calls starting next week.
  - *How I'll measure my success*: After I've listened to several calls, ask the VP if I can create an agenda for, and give project status on, an upcoming call.

Increase your commitment to your goals by writing them down in a list, and then sit down with your boss to review it and ask for his feedback. Do your personal goals align closely with your company's goals or the goals your boss has set for you? Are your boss's expectations practical given your level of experience and expertise? Are your own expectations reasonable? For example, does your boss concur with your goal to manage a client relationship self-sufficiently within six months, or does he feel that you'll require an additional year of mentoring before you'll be ready to take on that responsibility? Don't leave this initial meeting until you and your boss have agreed on your goals leading up to your first scheduled performance review. He will be impressed with your conscientiousness, and voilá—you'll be on the path to that promotion months sooner than if you'd waited for the formal review process.

Types of goals vary, depending on the specific job. Every twenty-something should aim to build a wide range of transferable skills (such as communication, interpersonal, and problem-solving skills) that will add value in any corporate job and that are not likely to become obsolete. I'll cover all of these skills in this book (it's a good idea to incorporate them into your goals). Use your time on the job and your company's resources to achieve goals related to transferable skills, even if such goals are not directly related to your daily job responsibilities. My friend Joanne wanted to move from her position as a research coordinator to a sales representative, and provided the following example:

- **Transferable Skill:** Communication.
- **Goal:** Improve presentation ability.
  - *What I'm going to do*: Teach three internal training courses about Microsoft Office.
  - *Why I want to do it*: I want to practice speaking in front of a group so that when I move to a sales rep position next fall, I will be qualified to conduct client presentations without supervision.
  - *When I'm going to do it*: Over the course of one training semester (six months).
  - *How I'll measure my success*: I'll work with the training coordinator to compare my evaluation sheets from the first and third courses. I'll know that I was successful if my scores improve.

Even after you've learned the basics, practice honing existing skills and acquiring new ones. Professional development never stops if you want to stay marketable. Keep a running list of all the job responsibilities you have and the projects you work on, and create a portfolio of work samples. Learn all you can about your company and your field.

Because developments in the corporate world move at the speed of the Internet, spend a few minutes each day reading Websites focused on your company and industry. Regardless of your position, keeping your finger on the pulse can only help you.

Independent of your manager's involvement, you should take the time to evaluate your goals and reflect on your progress every three to six months. Mark Swartz, a career columnist for the *Toronto Star*, recommends taking a regular inventory of what's working and what's not. Ask yourself the following questions and answer honestly:

- Are my current goals still valid?
- Have any new goals emerged?
- Are my priorities still in order?
- Have new priorities changed the emphasis of my efforts?
- Do my planning and daily activities support my goals?
- Am I on the right track to get where I want to go?

Finally, be positive. Focus on how far you've come instead of how far you have to go. Take time out to pat yourself on the back. Eat your favorite dessert, buy the better seats at a baseball game—whatever—as long as it's a real treat. By acknowledging your progress toward reaching your goals and concentrating on how close you are to achieving them, you'll be more likely to go the distance.

Earning Your Keep

When I was an account coordinator at a financial consulting company, there wasn't much I could do to help the senior members of my team close new business. But then, one night, I went to a dinner party that my mother was throwing for some of her friends. One of the guests had just gotten divorced and was looking to overhaul her portfolio. When she mentioned this, I saw an opportunity and recommended my firm. Back at the office, I made sure one of our senior reps followed up, and this woman was so impressed with our response and ideas that she hired us to do all of her financial planning. It turns out this woman was quite well-off, so a little effort on my part turned into a lucrative piece of business for my firm.

Melanie, 25, Arizona

If you're reading this chapter, chances are you're blazing a trail of ambitious fire. You probably can't wait to make your mark on the company and prove to everyone you're worth 10 times what they're paying you. Well, hold on there, partner. Taking initiative in order to add value is an excellent idea, but there are a few things you'll want to consider first.

At a new job, size up the turkey before you carve yourself a piece. Realize that no one is expecting you to make a sizable impact within a month of your start date. Actually, going out of your way to make a big splash could be perceived as presumptuous and might incite jealousy among your new colleagues. You should also assess your boss's personality before you jump right in on projects. Although most managers appreciate independence, some like to maintain tighter control over the group's work and will be insulted and/or threatened if they feel you're taking *too much* initiative. Bottom line: When looking for ways to prove your worth, you'll be safest if you start small.

Ask yourself what your company or department needs, and think about how you can use your unique set of skills and talents to provide it. So what if you're hardly a Renaissance man or woman? You're still new blood. Can you offer a fresh perspective on a vexing problem that has been plaguing your managers for months? Can you improve on an existing process or invent a new and more innovative one? Can you find a way to do something faster and more efficiently?

When I started a job in corporate communications, I discovered that my company lacked templates for certain documents, such as launch plans and activity reports. My colleagues weren't against the idea of creating templates— they'd just never thought of it. They created every new document from scratch because that was the way they'd always done it. I recognized that I could make a contribution by introducing the templates I used at my last job. However, I didn't want to appear as though I was forcing my methods upon my new company, so I started by casually incorporating the templates into my individual projects. Eventually, my teammates figured out on their own that the templates were huge productivity-savers. Instead of feeling offended or threatened, my colleagues and manager began to see me as an asset.

Even if you've been with a company for a while, never stop trying to add value. You have to give your company more than you take out in salary and benefits to be considered a worthwhile investment. In the financially-driven corporate world, it's not about effort—it is all about results, so you're better off concentrating on areas that directly impact your company's bottom line. Bruce Tulgan, founder of Rainmaker Thinking, Inc., recommends focusing on opportunities that present themselves, even if they're outside your official job description. For example, you might not be in sales, but you can help your company generate new business just by talking to people about what you do. You networked your way into the job, now go out and do it on behalf of your company!

Ownership

A few years ago, I attended my company's annual staff meeting. The CEO tossed a beach ball into the audience, and everyone watched for 5 minutes as the ball was batted back and forth. Finally, the CEO called for quiet and asked for the ball to be returned to him. He held it in front of us for a moment before speaking again. "I'm going to throw this ball again," he finally said. "And this time I want someone to catch it and hold onto it. I want you to treat this ball as if it were one of our customers. Instead of passing the inquiry to another person, own the issue yourself."

"Beach ball management"—or bouncing a request over to a colleague because it's not your responsibility to handle it—is all too common in the corporate world. I think e-mail forwarding was invented for this purpose. If someone asks you a question and you don't know the answer, make it your business to find it. I realize it's easier to pass on the request and forget about it, particularly if the person asking is not someone you need to impress or if the request has nothing to do with your area. But if you take that extra step to ensure your department or company is perceived in a positive light, you will add value and stand out as a team player.

Sometimes when you answer the phone, an exasperated coworker or customer will be on the line. Quite possibly, you will be the fourth or fifth person this individual has been transferred to during a single call. Don't underestimate the importance of being the one who actually offers assistance and shepherds the issue through to a satisfying resolution. All it takes is one grateful person to e-mail your boss expressing appreciation for your efforts, and your reputation is made. If that isn't enough of a reason to do a good deed, consider the corporate "karma" factor: Go out of your way to help someone today and the universe's system of checks and balances will see to it that you are rewarded later.

Of course, it's also imperative that you take ownership as it pertains to your job. Volunteer to take on tougher assignments whenever you can, and if you don't have much on-the-job experience yet, scout out small tasks that you can own. Treat every person you deal with as though he or she is your most important customer, and make sure to finish every project you start. If you encounter roadblocks, marshal your resources to get around them rather than letting a project languish. If a task requires you to follow up at a later date, stay on top of it and keep it on your calendar until it has been completed. You should never hear your manager say, "Whatever happened to that...?" Provide her with frequent updates so that she doesn't have to ask you for a status. You'll advance much more quickly when you can demonstrate the ability to manage projects with minimal supervision.

Who Knows What You Do?

> I wasn't promoted, because I worked too hard, if you can believe that. I was so busy that I stayed in my cube all day, every day. People would come by to talk, but I was so consumed by what I was doing that I usually brushed them off. I didn't tell anyone what I accomplished because I thought it was obvious. One day my boss resigned and the head of the department gave the open position to a girl whose productivity was at least half of mine. When I got up the guts to ask why, I realized that the big boss wasn't aware of half the things I did. All he knew was that I kept to myself and wasn't perceived as a team player.
>
> Claude, 28, Quebec

In Chapter 1, I talked about the necessity of showcasing your abilities and achievements in the business world, and suggested that you think of yourself as a publicist with the sole task of promoting *you*. It was easier to do this while you were interviewing, because all eyes were on you and you had your superiors' undivided attention. However, now that you are ensconced in a corporate job, people are not as inclined to listen, and you have to compete with all kinds of noise to be heard. It's no longer enough to keep your nose to the grindstone and turn in a solid day's work. If you want people to take notice of you and consider you a serious player, you must make your accomplishments visible.

This is not an easy thing to do, especially given what you were told over your 16 years of schooling. In high school and college, achievement was an individual endeavor. You were taught a lesson, you studied, you took a test, you got a score—and no one was the wiser. In fact, you were probably not encouraged to share your grades, particularly if they were good. You were equally successful, whether anyone realized it or not. The corporate world, however, is a whole different ball game. Your promotability depends not on *what* you do, but on *who knows* what you do. Being insular is most damaging at the lower levels of your career, when you are unknown to 99 percent of your company. You could be sitting at your cube churning out work like there's no tomorrow, but unless someone in a position of authority is aware of it, you probably won't get anywhere.

So how do you share your contributions without being perceived as arrogant or boastful? The key is enthusiasm. If you emphasize your passion when describing an achievement, people will think you're just excited about it. An excited person appears earnest, and it's hard to be critical of someone earnest. Practice on your boss. It's okay if you mess up and start bragging uncontrollably, because your boss is supposed to know about everything you're doing and can't fault you for keeping him informed. But when informing everyone else of your successes, be as subtle as possible. Here are a few tactics you can employ without leaving your desk:

E-mail Example #1:

Forward e-mails praising your work to your management, disguising them as modest FYIs and making the success seem as though it was a team effort (use "we" instead of "I"):

> **To:** Your Management
>
> **Subject:** Progress With Fab Client
>
> **Text:** FYI—looks as though we've made some good headway with Fab Client. Let me know how you'd like me to follow up. (Forwarded e-mail is below.)

E-mail Example #2:

Ask people outside your department who appreciated your stellar work to let your higher-ups know about it:

> **To:** Person Who Complimented You Effusively
>
> **Subject:** Thank You
>
> **Text:** Thanks so much for your kind words. You really made my day and I'm glad to be able to help. I know my manager, John Smith, would appreciate the input on how our group is doing. Would you mind sharing your feedback with him?

E-mail Example #3:

Disguise your own success through a thank-you note to others who worked on a particular project with you.

> **To:** Addresses of Those Who Worked On the Project
>
> **Subject:** Thank You
>
> **Text:** I wanted to take this opportunity to thank Stew and Sean for their hard work on our new business proposals this week. Due in large part to their efforts, my team was able to land two new clients—Fab Client A and Fab Client B. Congratulations to all!

You might feel weird the first few times you do something like this. Unless you have a major ego, deliberately trying to make yourself look good is not going to feel natural. But trust me, you'll get used to it. As a mentor of mine once said: Step out of your comfort zone often, and watch it get bigger every time.

One last point with respect to visibility: Always strive to share as many good ideas as you can. But, as a junior-level employee, you should be prepared that most of your suggestions will not be implemented. This is because, in the corporate world, most important decisions are made at a high level. You should not consider your visibility efforts a failure if your ideas are nixed before they see the light of day. The goal is to show the higher-ups in your department that you consistently make worthwhile contributions.

Risk-Taking

I'm not a big risk-taker myself, so it probably makes sense that much of this book is about treading carefully through the jungle that is the corporate world. However, there is a time and a place for everything, and I believe that if you learn to take calculated risks, you will be more personally fulfilled, and you will reap greater career rewards in a shorter period of time. Research cited in Gail Sheehy's book *Pathfinders* supports this point, suggesting that most truly contented people have taken substantial risks at some point in their careers.

Career author Harry Chambers defines risk-taking as the willingness to confront problems, recommend appropriate actions or solutions, and take responsibility for the ultimate outcomes. When you're a low man on the totem pole, putting in your two cents about anything may seem like a risk. You also have to be careful not to step on your colleagues' toes. For example, if your boss is around to handle a situation that falls under her jurisdiction rather than yours, chances are it's not appropriate for you to jump in and handle it for her.

When is a good time to take a risk that could jump-start your career? Because you can't plan for most opportunities (for example, your boss comes down with the flu and you must address a high-level executive's complaint in his absence), the best way to prepare is to learn in advance what would be considered an appropriate risk. This way, when you're presented with an opportunity in the midst of a stressful situation, you will be able to easily determine whether or not you should take the leap. Chambers suggests some risk-assessment questions to keep handy:

- What is the challenge?
- What is the potential upside? Will a positive outcome enhance your promotability?
- What is the potential downside? Would the worst-case scenario have a negative impact on your current or future promotability? How much risk are you comfortable with? Would a lack of success be a permanent hindrance or a bump in the road?
- How will you know if the risk starts to go bad? Will you be able to identify problems early enough to prevent career-damaging failure?
- How will you handle a negative outcome? What is your contingency plan if the risk isn't successful?

You will likely face stressful situations in your career, especially when a risk presents itself and you must act immediately. In his book *Feeling Better, Getting Better, Staying Better*, world-renowned psychologist Albert Ellis says that you can assuage your risk-taking fears by *preferring*, rather than *needing*, a successful outcome. Realize that a bad risk won't kill you. Sure you may lose, but you may also appreciably gain. Look at it this way: If you refuse to take risks, you will never get over your fear of them. Your career will be predictable and boring—and life is too short to live that way.

Also, keep in mind that how you react in a crisis tells others a great deal about you. If you're wishy-washy, you are likely to be perceived as ineffective, whereas if you take a confident stand, you will make a powerful statement about your career potential. Whatever you do, don't let on that you doubt yourself—nothing will cause people to lose respect for you faster. Even if you make a mistake, no one can fault you for courageously confronting a problem head-on. And when a plan doesn't work out, don't take it personally. A bad risk does not make you incompetent and shouldn't prevent you from taking similar actions in the future. Take stock of what went wrong and make a note to do it differently next time. There is no better way to learn.

Problem-Solving

My market research firm had so many ineffective processes, it was amazing we made any money at all. I thought I was being helpful when I showed my boss a spreadsheet detailing how many hours my colleagues and I wasted doing searches on the Internet. He immediately asked me what I proposed instead. I told him we should implement a software program to do the searches for us, but when he started in with more questions, I was at a loss. I guess I hadn't really thought it through. Looking back, I probably sounded like I was just complaining rather than actively looking for a solution to the problem.

Greg, 23, Massachusetts

As I've mentioned, knowing how to resolve issues and act decisively on the fly are skills you shouldn't be without. Early in your career, you may not have enough accountability to practice problem-solving on a regular basis, but if you take the time to master the process now, you will be all set when a curveball is thrown your way.

It's easy to say that a problem exists. Maybe you can even determine who's to blame. However, coming up with an effective solution is much more challenging, particularly when you're navigating uncharted waters. Problem-solving abilities do not come naturally to many people. Some are born procrastinators, and others become so stressed that they lose their ability to think rationally. Either way, when confronting a situation that requires action, many people put off addressing the issue until the window of opportunity has closed. If you are faced with a choice, it is usually more effective to take the wrong action than to do nothing at all. Managers expect twenty-somethings to make mistakes, so take advantage of this reality and look for opportunities to show what you're made of.

Let's look at the four steps of problem-solving with a potential scenario. Suppose it is just before Christmas. You work as a junior account executive at an advertising agency, and your client is a national bank. Your client contact informs you that the bank has had a sudden change in marketing management and wants your firm to pull together a presentation proposing some new creative campaigns. Unfortunately, the presentation is due just after the New Year, and your boss has already left for vacation. The future of an important client relationship is now in your hands. Yikes! What are you going to do? First, take a deep breath and don't let yourself get overwhelmed. You're going to solve this problem with a clear head, and you will come out looking like a superstar in the process. Here's how:

Step One: Define the problem in concrete terms.

What is the problem, specifically? In less than a week with most of the team on vacation, we must overhaul our existing advertising plans and devise a slide presentation detailing a new, yearlong creative campaign. I have neither the authority nor the expertise to create this presentation on my own.

Is this objectively a problem? Yes. I am not just panicking or exaggerating the criticality of this situation. The client really expects this presentation next week.

What can I gain by fixing it? This is a major opportunity to prove myself to senior executives in my firm and to develop a positive working relationship with my client without the interference of my managers.

Step Two: Generate as many possible solutions to the problem as you can.

What are the alternatives?

1. I could take the problem to the most senior executive in the office and let her handle it.

2. I could call my boss on vacation and explain the situation. Hopefully, she'll come back.

3. My boss recently experienced a similar crisis, and she brought in freelancers to do the job. I could find their contact information in her address book and call them in to help.

4. I could coordinate a brainstorming session with the more competent account managers in the office and use the ideas generated to formulate a presentable plan for senior management.

Are any of my potential solutions totally unrealistic? All of the options are realistic except for #3. At my level, I am not authorized to spend several thousand dollars to hire freelancers. I also cannot release control of the project to an external resource without senior executive approval.

Step Three: Evaluate each solution and choose the best alternative based on the pros and cons.

What are the pros and cons of Solutions #1, #2, and #4—my most viable alternatives?

> **Pros of #1:** Transferring responsibility on something of this magnitude is perfectly legitimate. I won't have to put myself out. I can go home and enjoy my time off.
>
> **Cons of #1:** The senior executive might not perceive me as a can-do person because I am coming to her with a problem and no potential solution. I will also make zero impact from a visibility perspective.
>
> **Pros of #2:** My boss is probably the best person to handle this situation. She has a long-standing relationship with this client, and she could probably do the job most effectively. Also, I would not be held personally accountable for the outcome.
>
> **Cons of #2:** Even though she'll understand, my boss might resent me for calling her during her well-deserved vacation. I will also lose the opportunity to showcase my problem-solving abilities and strong work ethic to my management and the client.
>
> **Pros of #4:** I could really increase my visibility and impress the office account managers and senior executives by effectively mobilizing resources in my boss's absence. It's possible that this incident will help me get promoted to account manager.

Cons of #4: I don't have a lot of experience with direct client interaction or creative campaign development, so it will be easy to make a mistake. Also, the account managers, the senior executives, and my boss might think I'm overstepping my bounds.

Have I prioritized the best option? After analyzing the pros and cons, I believe the benefits of #4 to be the most substantial, and its drawbacks to be the most tolerable. I can mitigate the risk by collaborating with others as I take the reins.

Step Four: Implement the chosen solution.

How will I roll out and communicate the solution?

1. I will coordinate an hour-long interactive brainstorming session with all of the account managers in the office.
2. I will organize the results of our session and put together a brief action plan.
3. I will present my recommendations to senior management and await a decision.

Have I developed a contingency plan? If things get out of hand, I can always pull in a senior executive to take over (see Solution #1). At least then everyone will know that I put forth my best effort.

●●●

Once the problem is yesterday's news, take a moment to assess how things worked out before you move on to the next big thing. If you succeeded, think about what worked and why, and document everything for later use in performance reviews or discussions about your goals with your manager. Don't forget to promote your success as subtly as you can and to sincerely thank the people who helped you along the way. Return the favor by sharing your skills and resources to help your colleagues with projects in the future.

If you didn't succeed, don't look at the experience as a failure. You simply made an ineffective choice. Your career is far from over, so dust yourself off and prepare for the next challenge. As I mentioned in the section on risk-taking, if you think about why you didn't succeed and try a different approach the next time, you'll be 100 percent on track. Take responsibility for the choices you've made, but don't overapologize. Believe in yourself and others will too!

Chapter 4 Take Home Points

✓ **Use your job to your advantage.** Acquire valuable skills and experience that will help you achieve your personal mission. Set specific, reasonable, and attainable goals for your present position that relate to your long-term career strategy.

✓ **Determine what they need, and make sure you can provide it.** Ask yourself what your company and department need, and think about how you can use your unique set of skills and talents to aid them. Look for ways to make your accomplishments visible to others.

✓ **Take appropriate risks.** Situations in which you have to act on the fly are excellent opportunities to prove your value. If you're indecisive, you are likely to be perceived as ineffective, whereas if you take a confident stand, you will make a powerful statement about your career potential.

✓ **Learn to resolve issues effectively.** Practice the four steps of problem-solving: Define the problem in concrete terms, generate as many potential solutions as you can, evaluate each solution, and choose the best alternative by weighing the pros and cons.

Chapter 5

The Purposeful Workday

Setting goals, generating visibility, solving company problems in the blink of an eye—these all sound great in
theory, right? But when you're a newbie in the corporate
world, you consider yourself lucky if you can just make it
through the day without dropping one of the 10 plates you
have spinning in the air. Besieged by a constant influx of
new assignments, it's unthinkable to even consider how
you're using your time. Forget about managing your career and monitoring your performance to achieve optimum
results. Some days, work seems so out of control that you
just want to put your head down on your desk and mutter
"uncle."

Wouldn't it be nice if you didn't have to live this way?
What if *you* ruled your schedule instead of the other way
around? What if *you* were the most effective person on
the team, not wasting any energy hating the colleague who
never misses a deadline or the one who always leaves the
boss's office with all of his questions answered? All of this
is totally possible if you take the time to develop a few new
habits. In this chapter, I'll cover how to make the most
out of the 8-plus hours a day you spend at work—from

effective time management and organization, to making every piece of communication count. Internalize these skills by reflecting on them outside the office when you have a moment to breathe and by planning how you can implement sanity-saving processes in advance. I think you'll find that the more proactive you are in managing your workday, the more you will actually achieve—without losing your hair or your bathroom breaks!

Where Has All the Time Gone?

It took me a long time to get out of the mode of thinking that a corporate job is like school. When I first started working, I treated everything like an assignment I would be graded on. I had no choice but to complete whatever was asked of me because I would 'fail' if I didn't. Eventually, I realized that I couldn't possibly do it all, and that I was going to have to prioritize if I was going to survive. Some things are just meant to slip under the radar. After all, if a task is relatively unimportant and no one will notice if it isn't done, is it really worth burning out over?

Leslie, 25, Ohio

It's impossible for one human being to do it all, and unless you want to spontaneously combust before the age of 30, you shouldn't try to. If you're thinking that you don't have any say in how you spend your time at work, consider whether this is a subjective state of mind or an objective reality.

Is your boss really watching you every second of every day? Probably not—he's got his own work and schedule to manage. I don't care if you're inundated with assignments that could potentially keep you busy for the next decade, the only person who can truly control your schedule is you.

Here's the thing: Struggling to get through each day by running frantically from one task to the next won't bring happiness or job satisfaction. You'll be exhausted, stressed, and unmotivated, and you won't have accomplished much in respect to your long-term career goals. For the first year of my career, I was so fried that you could see my hair crackling with electricity. I was so anxious for every senior person to like me that I accepted assignments indiscriminately—like a dog scarfing down table food. Boy, was I earning my $25K salary! I thought that all those days of nonstop agita would certainly earn me a promotion, so naturally I was surprised when I was passed over. At the time, I didn't understand that in the process of doing 7 million unrelated and unimportant tasks, I had neglected my professional development and hadn't acquired the core skills I needed to move to the next level.

As a general rule of thumb, you must manage your time strategically if you want your efforts to translate into personal fulfillment and career advancement. You can do this by organizing your schedule around your priorities. What makes a task a priority? Think back to the personal mission statement from Chapter 1 and the goals you set in Chapter 4. For the most part, your priorities should focus on results and relate back to your master plan. Here's an example: My friend Lou's personal mission has always been to live on a farm, but he went to school for hotel management. When Lou started his first job as a hotel front desk attendant, his goal was to develop the skills and knowledge base needed to manage his own country inn. In keeping with this goal, Lou made it a priority to interact with and learn from the Guest Services staff. Several years later, Lou is living on a farm, and the visitors to the country inn he runs pay the mortgage. By leveraging his hotel experience, Lou was able to achieve his long-term vision.

Focusing on tasks that contribute to your big picture sounds like a good idea, but how do you do it? Let's look at the approach advocated by Stephen Covey, author of *The 7 Habits of Highly Effective People*. To paraphrase Covey, there are four types of tasks:

✓ **Category 1:** Urgent and important tasks that allow you to keep your job (crises, deadlines, pressing problems).

✓ **Category 2:** Nonurgent and important tasks that allow you to develop professionally and work toward a promotion (relationship building, new skill acquisition, opportunity assessment).

✓ **Category 3:** Urgent and nonimportant tasks that allow you to maintain your reputation as a team player (interruptions, certain e-mail and phone calls, certain meetings, certain administrative work for senior team members).

✓ **Category 4**: Nonurgent and nonimportant tasks that will get you fired if you're not careful (busywork, shooting the breeze with colleagues, time-wasting activities).

By "urgent," Covey means that the task is highly visible and insists on action. An important task is relevant to your personal mission and corresponding goals. If you've been spending your days running around like a chicken with its head cut off, you are probably spending 90 percent of your time in Categories 1 and 3, and you might have noticed totally irresponsible people who hang out permanently in Category 4. When you master effective time management, you stay out of Category 4 and decrease the time spent in Categories 1 and 3 to allow more time for Category 2. Do this on a regular basis by scheduling time each week to achieve Category 2 tasks that relate to your goals, leaving space for unanticipated Category 1 and Category 3 activities. Review your schedule every day and take the time to reassess it, if needed. Remember to be flexible, because, unfortunately, life doesn't always work out the way you plan, and people often don't behave consistently.

You'll feel more on top of things if you keep a running "to do" list. Mentally separate all of your tasks into their respective categories, and then decide which ones you can eliminate, delay, or delegate. As you undertake a Category 1 or 3 task, think about how you can achieve the maximum impact with the least amount of effort. Remember to keep your department's processes and your own work style in mind. For example, if your group has status meetings every Tuesday morning, you might want to schedule your personal preparation for late in the day on Monday so that you can be prepared to deliver the most up-to-date information. Alternatively, if you are a morning person and your energy is highest just after you wake up, maybe you can slot an hour before office hours on Tuesday to organize your material.

When you're an overworked and underpaid junior member of your company, it's easy to fall prey to low morale. However, by developing strong time-management skills and focusing on tasks that will help you attain your long-term goals more quickly, you'll be able to approach each new day with a sense of purpose.

Saying No

By virtue of our low rank in the organizational hierarchy, we twenty-somethings are responsible for meeting the needs of the many individuals who supervise us. Work rolls downhill from all the people above us, and lands in a giant heap on our plates. Many older—but not necessarily wiser—managers have no qualms about piling it on and watching an eager-to-please twenty-something scramble around like a rat in a maze. Well, even if you're an efficient multitasker, you're never going to be Superman. Don't sabotage your goals by taking on more work than you can do just because someone asks you to. Staying true to the priorities we talked about in the last section means learning to say no sometimes.

No is a tricky word in corporate business, because you always want to be perceived as a can-do employee. In general, you should try to preempt situations in which you will have to decline an assignment. A good first step is to formalize your daily responsibilities with your official boss. Find out who on your team is authorized to delegate work to you, and note the type of assignments you can expect from each person. Let's say that Joe, who is outside this core group of delegators, gives you stack of expense reports to process. How should you respond? It's perfectly appropriate to politely reply that you would be glad to help, but that you would appreciate it if Joe would check with your manager first. Joe may or may not pursue the matter, but, either way, you have extricated yourself from an awkward situation and have placed the ball squarely in your boss's court. In all likelihood, your boss will say *no* to Joe for you, especially if processing expense reports is outside your area of responsibility.

Now imagine that Jane, a member of your core group of delegators, leaves an urgent assignment on your chair that must be done by the end of the week. Jane has known about the task for a few days, but now it's Friday morning and the deadline is looming. As my mother used to say, don't let another person's lack of planning become *your* emergency. If your own "to do" list dictates you do something else, speak up. Tell Jane that you wish you could do the task for her, but you are currently working on a project with Tom that requires your attention. Give her the option of resolving the issue with Tom or your boss, and emphasize how much you enjoy working with her. Ideally, Jane will leave the interaction with the perception that you sincerely do want to help her, but that you can't help being caught between conflicting responsibilities.

What if your boss is the one with an urgent request that you don't have the time to attend to? In a way, this is the least painful scenario, because all you really have to do is ask her to help you prioritize your various assignments. You can say something such as, "I'd be happy to take care of that, but today I'm researching statistics for Tom's client presentation. Which do you think I should do first?" If your boss wants to snatch your time at Tom's expense, that's her prerogative. Again, though, you have made someone else accountable for deciding which of the competing tasks you should direct your energy toward. Note that in all of these cases, you have declined to take on a new task. However, the actual word *no* and the phrase *I don't have time* are absent from the conversation. Always strive to present yourself as a hardworking and disciplined employee with the best interests of the department and company at heart.

One last point: Subscribing to the servant mentality is not good time management, even if you're not preoccupied with any urgent tasks. When you get into the habit of springing into action the moment a higher-up appears at your desk, people will come to expect that you are always available. Suddenly your delegators won't think twice about asking you to do all kinds of Category 3 (urgent and nonimportant) tasks. Meanwhile, Category 2 (nonurgent and important) priorities, such as professional development and on-the-job training, will slip farther and farther down your "to do" list. Remember, in the big-picture scheme of things, Category 2 should be *ahead* of Category 3, so no matter how busy your department is, always make time in your schedule for Category 2 activities. Have trouble doing this? Take note of the time it takes you to complete Category 3 assignments. For example, if you think it will take you an hour to run a database search for your boss, tell him you'll have it done by the end of the day. Also, instead of asking for new work the second you encounter a few free hours, spend some quality time researching your company's products, participating in on-site training, or meeting with your mentor (Category 2 activities). It's probably long overdue.

It might be difficult to turn your back on a Category 3 task that's presented to you or to set aside company time for your own Category 2 needs. But think about it this way: You have to say no to something. It's either the nonimportant or the important things. You decide.

Battling Procrastination

We all procrastinate in one way or another. Just because something is worth doing doesn't mean it's easy to get started. Even at work, we're constantly tempted by activities that are more fun and take less effort, such as chatting with a coworker or surfing the Internet. However, when you're trying to stick to a schedule of prioritized tasks, repeated procrastination can wreak havoc on your master plan. It may start with a simple decision to take a longer lunch instead of making headway on your first business plan, and, next thing you know, your goals are taking longer to achieve and your upward mobility has slowed to a crawl.

To fight this battle and win, you first must acknowledge that you are procrastinating. Did you actually schedule time to play Solitaire, or are you just putting off doing work? Confront the procrastination demon head-on and ask yourself why you're avoiding the task. Could it be that the task isn't worth the effort? Maybe the benefits of completing the task don't outweigh the time and energy you'll spend on it. If this is the case, reconsider whether it's a priority. Should you decide that the task *is* important, however, now is the time to rally your sense of discipline and get moving. The following are reasons you might use to put off work. Arm yourself with the following motivational arguments I have provided, and begin the battle against procrastination:

1. **You can do it later.** Think about whether a momentary reprieve is worth having to overhaul your whole calendar to reschedule a particular task. Do you want to repeat this same dance again later, or would you rather just get the task over with now?

2. **The task is boring and you'd rather do something fun.** Think about the big picture. Sometimes the most worthwhile activities require the most effort and, in turn, produce the greatest rewards. Besides, how can you really have fun when you're feeling guilty about blowing off your work?

3. **You're afraid the task will be too hard or take too long.** Consider that every minute you

spend procrastinating is one minute you could be using to complete the task at hand. Instead of looking at the task as a neverending dark tunnel, break it up into a series of short, manageable assignments, and think about resources you could call on for help at each stage.

4. **You don't know where to start.** Choose the least complicated part of the task, and work at completing it as swiftly and efficiently as possible. Once you've successfully finished one component, you'll gain momentum. The task will no longer seem like such a bear, and it will be much easier to move to the next component.

Don't forget to reward yourself for beating procrastination and finishing a task. Instead of moving on to the next assignment right away, block out time to do something you enjoy. Long hours of hard work will pass by much more easily when you can anticipate a fun activity at the end of the process. As I was writing this book, for example, I'd tell myself that each time I finished a section, I would spend a few hours watching a Lifetime movie on cable or playing the computer game *The Sims*. We all have our mindless vices. Remember Jack Nicholson in *The Shining*? All work and no play makes Jack a dull (not to mention *psychotic*) boy. So if you've earned it, go ahead and indulge!

You, Too, Can Be the "Organized One"

With the help of Microsoft NetMeeting, I became a pro at scheduling meetings for my team, which was dispersed across the country in four different offices. Somehow I thought that a meeting equaled progress on a project. It took me about five meetings to realize that we were always discussing the same topics, but never making decisions or creating action plans around any of them. It was like the clock had stopped. No matter how much we talked, we never accomplished anything. The meetings were actually a huge productivity drain because they took up so much time that they prevented us from getting our individual work done.

Seth, 27, Texas

Have you ever noticed that the most stressed-out folks at work are habitually disorganized? In their defense, it's easy to lose track of an important document, project, or deadline when you have hundreds of e-mails arriving every day and your paper inbox is flooded with swanky brochures that have nothing to do with your job function. However, there are only so many things in corporate business that you can control, and the way you organize is one of them. When you're organized, you're more confident, efficient, and dependable. You're also much less likely to be forced into early retirement by a heart attack or a nervous breakdown.

Before I launch into a discussion of ways to preserve your sanity by incorporating organization into your daily routine, let me admit something. I do tend to believe that organization is one of those pesky inherited traits. If you have it, it's likely that you've had it all along, and you probably skipped ahead the second you saw this section's header.

If you don't, these suggestions might not be as easy to implement as they sound. Take heart, though. If you can take one thing away from this section and use it to become more effective at work, reading it will have been worthwhile.

In Chapter 2, I talked about utilizing good organizational skills as you begin a new job, and I recommended starting at home base—your desk. To briefly recap, please do not buy into the misconception that an Armageddon of a cubicle makes you look super busy and hardworking. Remember that the corporate world judges performance by results, not effort, and your managers will doubt that you can achieve such results in the midst of total chaos. For those of us in a constant state of information overload, keeping a neat workspace requires vigilance. I suggest thinking of every new item arriving on your desk as an insect that is infiltrating your territory. Your job is to dispose of it as quickly as possible, either by chucking it in the nearest recycling bin or putting it in its proper place. The only material on your desk should pertain to the task you're working on at that very minute. Everything else should be labeled and filed for easy access.

Treat your e-mail inbox the same way. Delete spam and other messages you don't need as soon as they pop in, and if you know you have to respond, get in the habit of doing so immediately. When you receive a new task via e-mail, don't let it linger. Add it to your master "to do" list. Should a message require follow-up at a later time, flag it, and place it in a subfolder that you review on a daily basis.

I'm frustrated with a few people I work with who don't read their e-mail and always seem to be unavailable. I've tried everything from tagging messages with read receipts, to automatically resending messages that bounce back with one of those cheerful "Out of the Office" replies. I'm sure these e-mail neglecters have their reasons, but think about this: If I know they're not staying on top of their mail, other people, including their managers, must know it too. Even if these people haven't been seriously burned yet, their reputation is being compromised as we speak. Don't get tripped up by this one. Unless you're on vacation or physically unable to get to a computer, make it your business to check (and read) your e-mail several times a day.

Jumping on the paperless workplace bandwagon is another good way to enhance how you organize. Take advantage of a personal digital assistant (PDA), software tools such as Microsoft Project and Excel, or online content management systems. If you have Microsoft Outlook, you can set automatic task reminders to alert you to upcoming deadlines. Don't want to drag your laptop to meetings? You should still keep all of your notes in one location (such as a three-ring notebook or legal pad) rather than relying on a combination of loose sheets of paper and yellow Post-its. The key to making a routine stick is to find a system that works for you—the simpler the better!

Project Management

Several twenty-somethings have told me that they have difficulty coordinating projects with multiple tasks and individuals involved. Learning to do this well is a prerequisite for getting ahead in the corporate world. I have a few years of project management experience under my belt, and here's my strategy:

Step One: *Outline*

As soon as I leave my boss's office with a new mission, I consider the scope of the project and the general approach I want to take. I then create a rough outline that breaks the project down into smaller component parts.

Step Two: *Initial Project Meeting*

Conducting an initial project meeting allows me to turn the assignment of tasks into a team activity. By brainstorming with my teammates about the best way to accomplish various phases of a project, I encourage them to approach the work with enthusiasm and commitment. Note that team meetings should not be called indiscriminately. As much as I love the people I work with, if I want to hang out and chitchat, we'll go to happy hour. Remember that the real project work gets done outside the conference room and that, most of the time, you do not accomplish things simply by talking about them. In general, I don't usurp an hour of my colleagues' time unless the meeting will serve a combination of the following purposes:

- Generates ideas that will result in appropriate project strategy.
- Delegates each required task so that every member of the team is personally accountable for something.
- Provides status updates so that one hand always knows what the other is doing, and so that problems and delays can be flagged before they get out of hand.

Step Three: *Project Chart*

After an initial project meeting, I use Microsoft Project or Microsoft Excel to develop a horizontal bar chart that displays timelines, the interrelationships of the various tasks, and the people responsible for each project component. I check the chart once a day to monitor our progress and keep track of pending deadlines.

Step Four: *Communication*

In order to organize a project successfully, you must make it easy for your team members to communicate with each other. My chart, which sits on a shared server, is a living document. Everyone on the team, including my supervisor, has access to view and modify the chart as we move forward on various tasks. The chart, along with ongoing status reviews, ensures that every team member understands not just his or her own responsibilities, but everyone else's as well.

•••

Whether you're an experienced project manager leading a huge team or an entry-level assistant in charge of a single intern, look for ways to implement and showcase your own organizational strategies and tools. By inspiring trust, confidence, and cooperation, you'll emerge as an effective leader poised for even greater things.

Making Yourself Understood

Many people assume that communication is common sense and that there's nothing to learn about it. A manager, for example, wouldn't dream of sending a new employee on a client visit without providing in-depth training on *what* the employee should talk about. However, that same manager will most likely ignore the specifics of *how* the rep should speak to the client. Sounds pretty dumb, huh? After all, if the employee doesn't communicate effectively with the client in the first few minutes of interaction, he might have the door slammed in his face before he has a chance to recite his product's compelling features. Corporate business is the same way. You could be the smartest, most qualified employee in the company, but no one will care what you have to offer if you're unable to make yourself understood. So how do you ensure that your communication style is a competitive advantage rather than a liability? I'll get to that soon. But first, let's dissect a few types of communication found in the business world:

- **Aggressive:** Communication that infers blame, places responsibility for a bad outcome on the other person, and takes credit for any and all successes. The aggressive communicator discourages collaboration and cooperation.
- **Passive:** Communication that does not convey the whole picture. The passive communicator shares information with reluctance, fails to offer feedback, and responds with blanket agreement—particularly at the first sign of confrontation.
- **Assertive:** Communication that is non-accusatory, nonjudgmental, and conversational in tone. Assertive communicators are in control of themselves. They think before responding, avoid personalizing problems, and consider the big picture.

I'm sure you've had the pleasure of interacting with plenty of aggressive and passive communicators. Maybe some of them were lucky enough to advance to a high level. Usually, though, these extreme styles will handicap a career because people don't respond well to them. If you have your eye on a VP position and want to be seen as a powerful communicator and a key influencer, assertiveness—or the ability to stand up for your rights, opinions, ideas, and desires, while respecting those of others—is the way to go.

Let me confess that I am not naturally the most assertive person in the world—I definitely lean more toward the passive style. Though I hate to admit it, I think it has something to do with growing up as a female in our society.

Women are encouraged to be passive from early childhood up until we're thrust into the corporate world, when we're promptly expected to grow a backbone. Fortunately, communicating assertively on an everyday basis is pretty easy provided you willingly express yourself clearly, confidently, and in a conversational tone that sounds friendly rather than fake.

It's harder to be assertive when you move beyond small talk into the realms of persuasion and confrontation. In situations where you must communicate your point to someone who doesn't agree, assertiveness makes the difference as to whether you are perceived as a leader or as one of those "ineffective" or "difficult" people that populate the lower ranks of corporate business. Hendrie Weisinger, author of *Emotional Intelligence at Work*, makes the following suggestions for incorporating assertive communication into your problem-solving technique:

- Use facts to justify your position.
- Acknowledge that you understand the other person's point of view.
- Repeat your position (be consistent and don't raise your voice).
- Communicate emotion by using *feeling* statements (for example, "I feel disappointed that you are not comfortable assigning me this project") rather than *accusatory* statements (for example, "You don't trust me to work with your clients") that express an opinion as a matter of fact.
- Strive for a compromise.

Plan for important conversations ahead of time. Assertiveness does not just mean opening your mouth each and every time you have an opinion. Before you speak, make sure you fully understand your *own* point of view, and think about the most appropriate way to communicate it. Also, it never hurts to take an extra minute to decide whether or not something should be shared. When in doubt, err on the side of caution.

Watch people around you who are using assertiveness to their advantage. *Toronto Star* career columnist Mark Swartz recommends choosing a few role models in the office, and noting the behaviors they use to communicate effectively. Why does your coworker always seem to get the ear of your boss? How does your supervisor come out of every staff meeting with an increased budget for new projects? Try some of the successful techniques you see, keeping in mind that your communication style should match who you are personality-wise. If you stray too far from what comes naturally, you might be perceived as phony, and we don't want that!

Now that I've talked about the role of assertiveness, let's cover specific strategies for leveraging three communication vehicles—writing, speaking, and listening—to help you connect with people in ways that will enhance your career potential.

What You Write

I learned the hard way never to write anything in an e-mail that you wouldn't want to see on the front page of *The Washington Post*. I overheard my workmate talking to one of our colleagues about her recent divorce. She sounded really upset, so I wrote her an e-mail expressing my sympathy and telling her I could totally relate to her predicament. Unfortunately, I put in all the details of my own divorce, including my ex-husband's infidelity. I really wish I had just talked to her in person, because I accidentally sent that e-mail to the entire company. I have never been so mortified in my life.

Hilary, 29, Virginia

Word on the street is that if you're *not* a communications professional, you don't need to pay too much attention to your writing skills. This is not so. In fact, good writing is one of the most underrated skills in the corporate world. Maybe this attitude is a defense mechanism. After all, many businesspeople are bad writers, and how can you judge your employees on something *you* don't even have a clue about? If you're not the most polished writer in the world, you might very well get away with it. But you're not reading this book so you can just slide by. Presumably, you want to impress the socks off your managers and come out looking better than everyone else. There's no better way to do this than to showcase the rare talent of a superior command of the written language.

I could quite happily devote an entire book to the craft of writing. However, because that's not what I'm here to do, I'll limit my advice to two simple rules:

Rule #1: *C&C* (*Clear & Concise*). Most people in corporate business have a very short attention span. Get right to it by prefacing your document with a brief, objective-oriented introduction, and by setting off your key points with bullets for painless consumption. Whether you're writing a routine memo or a quarterly business plan, offer only the necessary information and be prepared to provide supplemental material. Your word choice should accurately convey your meaning, and your vocabulary and tone should reflect your audience.

Rule #2: *Quality Control*. There is no such thing as a perfect first draft, so get into the habit of proofreading your writing. Sloppiness is the enemy. Every document that leaves your desk should be carefully checked for clean formatting, proper grammar, and correct spelling. Think of your work product as little pieces of yourself sent out into the world. Even if you're the 15th person to review a document, be the one who takes responsibility for sending it forward error-free.

What if your business requires you to communicate with clients in a different language and/or you need some help bringing your writing up to par? I suggest contacting local colleges or continuing education programs about a variety of foreign language and business writing courses. Classes are typically inexpensive, and they can often be tailored to your specific needs. Don't let an inflexible schedule discourage you: Many courses are now offered over the Internet.

A lot of written communication now takes place through e-mail, which can be rather complicated. You still want to follow the C&C and Quality Control rules of regular written communication, but you also have to balance a multitude of considerations that are unique to the medium of e-mail. Used properly, e-mail can be a convenient and efficient tool that helps you get your job done 10 times faster. Just be aware of the pitfalls—and always think before you hit the Send button!

Allow me to share a true story. A student at a prestigious U.S. university was studying abroad, and e-mailed the dean of Undergraduate Affairs to determine the status of his Resident Advisor application. Because this particular student had been away all semester, the dean had forgotten to include his application in the pool. The student, having lost his opportunity to be a Resident Advisor, was quite upset. He shared his displeasure with the dean via e-mail. The dean became defensive. He intended to forward the student's e-mail to a colleague in the office, adding the comment, "What a little snot. These spoiled brats think they're entitled to everything. Why doesn't he just transfer?" Unfortunately, the dean accidentally hit reply, and the student received his nasty retort instead. No matter how much the dean apologized, the damage could not be undone. The already irate student had a field day distributing the dean's inappropriate and unprofessional response to everyone he knew, and, within a few months, the infamous e-mail exchange had made its way across the country. Ask yourself this question: How many e-mail offenses like this does it take to ruin a prominent university's reputation?

E-mail can be your best friend or your worst enemy. Here are a few tips to make it work for you:

Smart E-mail Communication Top 10

1. *Realize that e-mail is not private.* Not only can your company's IT department access it, but you never know who your messages might be forwarded to—accidentally or intentionally. Avoid discussing sensitive information or writing anything negative unless it's specifically requested by your boss and/or supported by fact.

2. *Maintain a consistent corporate persona.* You can achieve this by crafting friendly, polite, and grammatically

correct messages. Because you can't rely on voice or nonverbal cues, always reread your e-mails to make sure the message you are sending is idiot-proof.

3. *Keep e-mails short and to the point.* Make sure to include an informative and specific subject line (for example, don't just call the message "Update"). Begin with a call to action that encourages the person to read the message (starting with the word *you* usually does the trick). Put your key message up front, and if the information you must communicate is longer than 2–3 paragraphs, attach a Word document with the relevant details.

4. *Use e-mail to reinforce in-person conversations.* Impart helpful information (for example, *FYI*—or *"For Your Information"*—messages) or respond appropriately to an important issue (for example, *CYA*—or *"Cover Your Ass"*—messages) via e-mail to reinforce face-to-face discussions you have with colleagues.

5. *Don't use e-mail as a forum to express displeasure or criticize.* Do these things in person rather than taking the easy way out. If you must highlight a problem in e-mail, be positive and solution-oriented.

6. *Use e-mail sparingly.* Carbon copy (CC) your boss only on messages that clearly demonstrate that you are doing your job. Avoid sending him thousands of e-mails unless you want him to stop reading them.

7. *Use flags and read receipts.* When sending an important message to someone who you know is unreliable, increase your chances of a response by flagging the message or attaching a read receipt.

8. *Be courteous.* As a general rule, e-mailing a question to anyone sitting within 10 feet of you is considered rude. Speak to these people face to face.

9. *Know what you are sending before you send it.* Before hitting reply, carefully read an e-mail in its entirety. If it's preceded by a series of messages, make sure to read and understand the whole string first.

10. *Keep personal e-mails personal.* If you want to send personal e-mails at work, set up a separate account. Don't send those annoying forwards to your work friends unless they also qualify as real friends (see Chapter 3).

What You Say

I always keep my notepad handy when I go downstairs, in case I run into someone I need to talk to in the elevator. People in my company are so buried that it's nearly impossible to get them to respond to me via e-mail or voice mail. And forget about scheduling meetings. Cornering them in the elevator is the perfect opportunity to get quick answers so that I can do my job.

Steven, 26, North Carolina

Author and motivational guru Dale Carnegie once said that the person who can speak acceptably is usually considered to possess greater ability than he actually has. In my experience, this is true. If you look and act like you know what you're talking about, people will think that you do, regardless of the reality. You may not have a vast store of knowledge and years of experience to draw from, but you can get promoted just by creating the perception of being competent and informed.

I translate Carnegie's "speaking acceptably" as "effective in-person communication," because there is much more to speaking than the content that comes out of your mouth. Did you know that only 7 percent of meaning is conveyed with the words you say? People get the rest of your message based on *how* you say it. In-person communication includes nonverbal cues, vocal style, articulateness, and sincerity, and it plays a huge role in conveying the powerful corporate persona I talked about in the beginning chapters of this book. Let's spend a moment addressing each of these components:

1. **Nonverbal Cues:** Positive body language supports your message and encourages cooperation. Position yourself next to the person you're speaking to and lean toward him, but don't get so close that you invade his personal space. Sustain eye contact for several seconds over the course of the conversation, and always smile unless you're delivering bad news. Take the time to focus on the other person, and don't fidget or give in to background distractions. If you want to emphasize an important point, use your hands.

2. **Vocal Style:** Need something to do in the shower besides sing? Practice adjusting your tone, pace, and volume according to the situation and/or person with whom you are going to communicate. Enunciate your words so that people can understand you. Whether you are passionate about your subject or not, always convey a little enthusiasm—people will be more likely to listen.

3. **Articulateness:** Just as with written communication, practice your command of verbal communication so that you can accurately express what you mean. Improve your vocabulary in order to appear intelligent and well-educated, but don't overdo it. If you throw around too many industry terms or five syllable SAT words, you'll look like you are trying to impress someone. A huge part of articulateness is being succinct, so learn to communicate your main points using as few words as possible. This is particularly important if you regularly participate in meetings. There is nothing worse than being the one person who goes on and on while everyone else just wants to get out of there.

4. **Sincerity:** Note that there is a fine line between portraying a strong corporate persona and coming across as being fake. While your tone should generally be confident, friendly, and conversational, you should avoid saying things you don't mean or adapting a style that is completely contrary to your personality.

Voice mail is the perfect medium to work on your in-person communication technique. Your greeting serves as an introduction to the professional you. It is the starting point from which everyone—inside *and* outside the company—will communicate with you. That said, you have to nail it. Record your greeting before or after work hours to avoid office background noise. Politely and confidently state your name, department, and company, and invite the caller to leave a message, which you will promptly return. I would avoid saying what day it is in your message. I guarantee you will get behind in recording a new greeting each day, and, next thing you know, it will be October and your voice mail will still say it's June 5!

Public speaking is another good way to hone your in-person communication skills. Many of us fear getting up in front of a group, yet I've never known a person who was physically incapable of doing it after practicing a few times. Public speaking increases your confidence level, your poise, and your ability to flexibly convey information about your subject matter. It also pays huge dividends in terms of being taken seriously as a twenty-something in the corporate world. Nervousness is natural, but it shouldn't stand in the way of a substantial investment in your career. Look for opportunities to deliver formal or informal presentations whenever you can, and, as you prepare, consider using a few notes instead of a script. Extemporaneous remarks are more effective for connecting with your audience on a personal level and provide much better training for those critical one-on-one interactions.

Even if you're a master of in-person communication, people won't always welcome you in for a chat with open arms. As you well know, the corporate world is a hectic environment where no one has enough hours in the day to do what they need to do. The higher the executive's title, the less time she has to speak with you. Here are a few hints for getting face time with those hard-to-pin-down folks:

- Stop by her office instead of calling or sending an e-mail.
- Persuade her admin to give you a 10-minute slot on her calendar. (Make sure not to stay a minute longer.)
- Catch her for a quick conversation in the hallway or elevator.

- Invite her to have lunch in the cafeteria. (Everyone has to eat!)

Once you manage to get in front of the person, remember the Clear & Concise rule. Say what you have to say, and get out of there. If necessary, prepare a list ahead of time of the things you want to cover so that you can whiz right through them. If the person learns that a meeting with you doesn't mean she will be held up all day, she will be more likely to respond to your meeting request next time.

When You Listen

You may have taken one look at this subhead and said, "What am I, 5 years old? I thought I learned to listen in kindergarten!" If you think about it, though, this isn't exactly the case. You learned to hear people when they talk, but you didn't necessarily get into the habit of actively listening to them. In our corporate jobs, our relationships suffer, we miss out on a lot of information, and, ultimately, we make our jobs harder because we don't pay attention to what people are saying.

For obvious reasons, it's in your best interest to avoid unnecessary communication breakdowns caused by a failure to listen. Author Hendrie Weisinger recommends that you begin by making yourself aware of ways you might unconsciously filter out what others are saying. Filters are generated by thoughts, ideas, and feelings. They influence the *type of* and *how much* information we hear. There are four kinds of filters:

- **The *predilection* filter**: Hearing what you want to hear instead of what is meant.
- **The *who* filter**: Placing importance based on the person doing the talking.

- **The *facts* filter**: Being oblivious to the emotional subtext of the conversation.
- **The *distracting thoughts* filter**: Allowing your mind to wander.

Once you've identified what types of filters you use and under what circumstances you use them, employ these suggestions for practicing "filter prevention," and also for becoming an active and involved listener:

- Don't interrupt.
- Don't tune out because you think you know what's coming.
- Read between the lines, and assess what is meant vs. what is said.
- Acknowledge that you are paying attention by sustaining eye contact, nodding, or saying "uh huh."
- Verbally summarize what the speaker has said, paraphrasing rather than repeating it verbatim.
- Empathize with how the speaker is feeling.
- Ask specific, clarifying questions.
- Take notes to keep yourself focused and to help you remember what's being communicated.
- Don't change the subject until you're certain the speaker has concluded his or her point.

You can encourage others to listen to *you* by emphasizing key points, and by asking for a restatement of your message in the person's own words. Make your position relevant to the listener, and, as a general rule, listen more than you talk. You will stand out as one of the few people your colleagues consider it a pleasure to talk to!

Chapter 5 Take Home Points

✓ **Manage your time strategically.** Arrange your schedule around your priorities, and learn to say no to nonstrategic tasks in a way that maintains your persona as a can-do employee.

✓ **Implement effective organizational tools.** There are only so many things in the corporate world you can control, and your own organizational style is one of them. Find a simple routine that works for you, and stick to it.

✓ **Be assertive.** Become a powerful communicator and key influencer by standing up for your ideas, while also respecting those of others.

✓ **Fine-tune your writing, speaking, and listening skills.** Express your ideas confidently and succinctly. If you look and act like you know what you're talking about, people will believe that you do. Practice "filter prevention" in order to become an active and involved listener.

Chapter 6

Check Your Attitude
at the Door

The most disgruntled employees in today's companies are usually the twenty-somethings. Why? I think it's because the people running the corporate world are of a different generation. When we twenty-somethings were young, our parents told us we could be anything we wanted. They consumed a steady diet of "how to raise a happy, confident, socially skilled, psychologically stable, intellectually stimulated child" books, and lavished attention on us to compensate for their working while we were still in booster seats. As a result, we grew up feeling like we were the most special people in the universe. Educated on computers and the Internet, we learned rapidly or were left behind. Now that we're in the corporate world, we're innovative, entrepreneurial, and devoted to changing business for the better.

Although most managers would like to believe otherwise, corporate business doesn't always operate according to these values. In fact, the generation in power tends to believe that twenty-something employees would do the world a favor if we settled down, did our jobs, and resigned ourselves to living in the real world of corporate bureaucracy.

Naturally this frustrates us, and it's only too common for our companies to become a battleground of "us vs. them." Only guess what? *They* are in the driver's seat. When we're running the show, perhaps we'll do things differently, but we'll never get there unless we learn to work with the system, keep our differences of opinion to ourselves, and serve with a smile.

Because this can be more challenging than any skill we've discussed so far, I'm devoting an entire chapter to strategies for combating negativity, maintaining a positive attitude, and staying motivated in the face of difficult circumstances. By the time you move on to the next chapter, you will be armed with the most powerful weapon a twenty-something can possess in corporate business: the ability to harness the power of your own thinking and create a pleasant situation out of a maddening one.

No, You're Not Crazy

My department must hold the record for the company's fastest revolving door. In less than a year, we've been reorged three times. I've had four different managers, and every new person who comes in wants to 'mark his territory.' Meanwhile, none of these people know as much about my area as I do, so their guidance is useless. Plus, I'm changing direction so much I never get anything done. What is it they say—same sh*t different day? If I have to be 'rah rah' at yet another welcome lunch, I think I'm going to explode.

Robert, 27, Oregon

If you're reading this chapter because you're struggling with someone's attitude problem at work, you're not alone, and your hostility is probably justified. I've spoken to dozens of twenty-somethings, and most have spent their fair share of time banging their heads against the wall and regretting the day they signed their offer letters.

As much as I feel your pain, I don't believe it does much good to complain, because unless you're going to grad school, you're in the corporate world to stay. We all have to deal with business-world insanity whether we love our jobs or not, so we might as well take the necessary steps to overcome the challenges. However, because this chapter is about your emotional well-being, we need to start by recognizing the things about work that drive us nuts. Most of these points will probably sound familiar, so read on and be comforted. Warning: Do not hang this list in your cube!

Top 10 Annoying Things About the Corporate World

1. **Corporate Déjà Vu.** It seems as though it's a requirement in corporate business that you spend huge amounts of time reporting the same information in a dozen different formats, attending status meetings where conversation from the week before is repeated word for word, and putting out the same fires, because your department doesn't learn from its mistakes.

2. **Invoking Syndrome.** The invoking syndrome occurs when colleagues try to persuade you to do what they want by name-dropping someone higher up. Whether the executive manager was actually involved or not, invoking him is a manipulative tactic used to get you

to bend to your colleagues' wishes (for example, "Really? Well, I spoke to the CEO last night, and he told me we have to do the event this way.")

3. **Egomania.** When certain people reach a high level in a company, they think that they are better than everyone else and that they are entitled to be treated like a god. Regardless of the issue, they believe they are always right and that they can't possibly learn anything from someone lower on the chain.

4. **Hierarchies.** In the corporate world, all men are not created equal, and you can actually get in trouble just by talking to someone higher up without going through the proper channels. Unless you happen to know the right people, you're invisible.

5. **Denigration.** In most companies, it's an unspoken rule that the younger you are, the less respect you receive. Many senior managers are quick to call you on the carpet for situations that may or may not be your fault, but they say nothing when you've done superior work.

6. **Bureaucracy.** How many departments does it take to screw in a lightbulb? Corporate business has a lengthy approval process for *everything*, and companies delight in changing those processes constantly so that you're never sure which 10 departments you need to consult before a decision can be made.

7. **Hypocrisy.** Don't you just love the way some companies tout values such as quality, entrepreneurship, innovation, and integrity, when they would be perfectly happy if their employees just kept quiet and never strayed from their designated roles? If you've ever acted on your company's values and gotten burned for it, you are probably a victim of *naked ambition* (when doing what's best for the company leaves you out in the cold).

8. **Micromanagement.** Twenty-somethings thrive on independence, yet some managers will bear down on you with critical eyes at every minuscule stage of a project. Gotta sneeze? Better make sure your manager knows about it.

9. **Uncommon Sense.** I recently read that common sense is dead in the corporate world. The author almost sounded proud of this. People might make a joke of it, but this dearth of logical thought in corporate business is kind of sad. It's also frustrating when the obviously correct way to do something is staring everyone right in the face, and no one sees it.

10. **Nonsensical Change.** Every now and then, companies will decide to throw their departments up in the air and see where all the pieces land. Yes, it's the corporate reorganization (aka the dreaded *reorg*). Despite the fact that it results in mass confusion, greatly decreased productivity, and low employee morale, companies continue to do it year after year.

Combating Negativity

A week before one of our training seminars, our Group Manager announced that he was changing the curriculum. With one arbitrary decision, weeks of work were flushed down the toilet and we were left scrambling. When my boss told me the news, I thought I could actually feel my blood boiling. I should have gone outside to get some air, but instead I followed my boss into the Group Manager's emergency planning meeting. I was so pissed off at the guy for screwing everything up that I couldn't help showing some attitude. The Group Manager didn't say anything about it—he just kind of frowned. But afterwards, my boss had some words for me. He said that he thought I was more mature than that, and that I needed to learn some emotional control. So much for all the great work I did on the seminar.

Donovan, 27, Michigan

When one of the corporate world's realities frustrates you, you might want to stomp your foot and scream, "It's not fair! It doesn't make any sense! It's wrong!" Incident after incident convinces you that your managers are a bunch of crazy lunatics, and that every time you turn around, someone or something is keeping you from succeeding at work. You quickly develop a bad attitude without considering the consequences.

I fell into this trap at the beginning of my career. I had a clear mental picture of how the business world should operate, and I considered my company's inefficiencies to be a personal tragedy. Every time my progress toward my goals was blocked, my resentment grew (and I'm the type of person who wears my emotions on my sleeve). Pretty soon my managers didn't want to give me bad news because they were afraid of my reaction. I was probably one of the most capable people in my group at the time, but did I get promoted? No sir. I stayed exactly where I was and watched as coworkers with half my skills moved ahead of me. Eventually I quit, believing my company was the problem. Two jobs later, I realized that corporate business is the same everywhere, and that the problem was not my job, but rather my *attitude*.

Negativity might be a natural reaction to frustration, but that doesn't mean it's the right one. Pessimistic twenty-somethings waste a lot of energy being unhappy. They're unpopular with their colleagues because they suck the life out of everyone around them, and their corporate personas suffer because they are perceived as immature. One of my first managers used to say that a bad attitude is like cholera: The person who catches it is vocal in his misery and gives the plague to everyone around him before finally kicking the bucket. Unless you want your career to end prematurely, your strategy must be to kill negativity before it kills you.

Maintaining a positive attitude when faced with de-motivating situations is not easy, but it is under your control. I'm not suggesting that you suppress your bad feelings and walk around smiling when you really want to hurt someone. In fact, if you pay close attention to the suggestions in this chapter, you won't have to fake it at all. By learning to adjust your thoughts, let go of irrational expectations, and manage your emotions to banish anger, worry, and stress, you will genuinely become a happier and more peaceful person.

You Are What You Think

The Parable of the Three Neighbors

Three neighbors were standing in the road, talking about their possessions.

"I own a huge villa!" one said proudly.

"Oh yeah?" scoffed the second. "Well, I own a successful farm!"

"I don't have a villa or a big farm," the third said quietly. "But I do have optimism."

His two neighbors laughed at him. Optimism was hardly something to boast about, for what good is a possession that can't be seen or touched? Late that evening, the neighborhood experienced a violent storm. The rain destroyed the first neighbor's house. "What am I to do?" he cried, wringing his hands.

The wind ruined the second neighbor's crops. "I am finished!" he lamented.

The storm also destroyed the third neighbor's home and crops. "Well then, what should I do first?" he asked himself. After only a few minutes of consideration, he began rebuilding his home and replanting his crops. The next day, he whistled to himself as he went into his yard with some tomato seeds. His neighbors were still standing in the road feeling sorry for themselves. "We don't understand why you walk with a spring in your step," said the first neighbor. "All of your possessions have been destroyed."

"Yes," said the second. "What is your secret?"

"It is no secret," the man said. "The only thing I own is what I think."

•••

If you take away one thing from this chapter, let it be that your thoughts control your feelings and make you who you are. As a human being, you are responsible for your own life, and you have the ability to choose your response to your environment. Have you ever stayed late at work and noticed that at least half of the janitors are smiling and whistling as they go about their cleaning? Now, objectively, these folks might not have the most stimulating job in the world, but some of them make the decision to begin each day with a positive outlook. Fulfillment, my friend, is not about the job itself—it's about one's attitude toward the job. Nothing—and no one—controls your attitude but *you*.

You can change your attitude for the better by recognizing that you create your feelings with the thoughts you choose to concentrate on. Let's look at a few examples of how a person might react differently in a given situation, depending on if they choose to be negative or if they choose to be positive and productive:

Situation #1: *A less competent coworker receives a promotion over you.*

> **Negative Reaction:** "My boss is such a jerk. He doesn't know good work when he sees it."

> **Positive Reaction:** "I need to find out what I can do to receive the promotion next time."

Situation #2: *It's 5 p.m. on Friday, and you were just given a difficult assignment that's due Monday morning.*

> **Negative Reaction:** "There's no way I can do this. I can't believe they didn't give me more notice."

> **Positive Reaction:** "Let me think about what resources I can call on to get this done tonight, so that I can still enjoy my weekend."

Situation #3: *You're given a task that doesn't exactly fit your job description.*

> **Negative Reaction:** "I didn't sign up for this. I'm totally underqualified, and they're not paying me enough."

> **Positive Reaction:** "Maybe I can learn something new, and impress my boss in the process."

Situation #4: *You just found out that your company is only giving 2 percent raises this year.*

> **Negative Reaction:** "This is how they repay all of my hard work? They can afford an expensive holiday party, but they can't reward their best employees? This company sucks."

Positive Reaction: "The economy is pretty bad right now. At least I have a job I enjoy."

Notice that in all of these hypothetical situations, the negative reactions have some truth to them. Every situation has pluses and minuses. However, it's hazardous to your well-being to focus only on the minuses, even though they may be first to pop into your mind. Now don't get me wrong: Short-lived negative reactions such as concern, regret, disappointment, annoyance, and frustration are normal and often understandable. Rather, it's the negative reactions we hold onto—rage, panic, depression, self-pity—that wreak havoc over time, and eventually result in a bad attitude. To maintain a positive attitude over time, you have to make a conscious effort to throw constructive thoughts into the mix. You'll be happier, more productive, and more pleasant to be around.

The SHOULD Patrol

Like negative thoughts, irrational expectations can be an attitude-buster—not just in corporate business, but also in life in general. When we hold onto a belief that something *should* or *must* happen, we set ourselves up for inevitable disappointment. According to the prominent psychologists Marvin Goldfried and Gerald Davison, much of our emotional turmoil is, in fact, self-produced when we tell ourselves that our lives will be awful if a certain expectation is not fulfilled. Recognize any of the following?

- I *should* be able to do A...
- B *should not* happen to me...
- My company *should* do C...
- He *should* understand D...
- Everyone in this place *should* E...

- This project/campaign/event *should* be planned like F...

  ...or all hell will break loose!

If you catch yourself thinking or saying the word *should,* go directly to jail and do not collect $200! *Should* often signals that you're harboring an irrational expectation. As we've talked about, life does not always play out in a logical or fair way, and you do yourself a grave disservice when you hold on to a fantasy of what work or people should be like. A case of the *shoulds* can be downright dangerous if it leads you to freak out trying to correct a maddening situation that is beyond your control. You'll appear negative and panicky to your colleagues, and the situation won't turn out any better than it would have if you'd just stayed calm and dealt with the circumstances as best as you could.

Got a bad case of negativity? Remember that *all hell breaking loose* is in the eye of the beholder, and ask yourself if the world is really going to come to an end if things don't go exactly as you planned. Instead of thinking that something *should* happen, reframe it as something you *would like* to happen. You're still acknowledging your own opinions and preferences, but the element of expectation is gone, so you can't be disappointed.

Make a commitment to be more tolerant and flexible, and recognize that everyone has a different point of view. Instead of creating a whole bunch of rules and judgments based on your own ideals, walk into your office each day with an open mind. Whenever you can, think about how lucky you are to be educated, employed, and to most likely have a standard of living that is better than 97 percent of the world's population. You'll notice an improvement in your attitude overnight, without any changes in your work situation whatsoever!

The Positive Now

Most of us spend a great deal of time obsessing about the past, the future, and how we're going to use the people and things in our lives to get what we want. What if we recognized that every moment is potentially satisfying and inspiring in and of itself? After all, the most important moment in our lives is the one we're experiencing right now, for all others are either just a memory or don't yet exist. What if we could shut out negativity by becoming deeply involved in everything we do, every day?

Even if you start off the day with a positive frame of mind, your sense of well-being can fade as the hours wear on. Should you feel yourself slipping into unproductive modes of thinking, try the following:

- Consider how what you're doing relates to your big-picture goals.
- Get up from your desk and walk around or stretch.
- Think about ways to make a positive difference right now.

When you routinely exist in the moment, you become more conscious of how you behave around others and how certain situations affect you. This comes in handy for coping with negative emotions that rear their ugly heads at work. In the next section, I'll talk more about how you can develop your emotional intelligence to effectively fight attitude-busters such as anger, worry, and stress.

Reach Out and Touch Your Emotions

Most of us have taken an IQ test at some point or another, but you've probably never given your *EQ* a second thought. Author and psychologist Hendrie Weisinger

explains that EQ, or emotional intelligence, means intentionally using your emotions to guide your behavior. For
example, let's say your boss just told you that his budget
has been cut and your pet project must be canceled. In
this situation, it's likely that negative emotions would overwhelm you. Without even thinking, you might fly off the
handle and lash out at your boss. When you've honed your
EQ, however, you immediately stop and consider how this
development has made you feel. Once you've ascertained
that you're angry, you might prevent your emotions from
spilling over by talking yourself through them or taking a
time-out.

Achieving Self-Awareness

High self-awareness is the basic building block of EQ.
Think of it as stepping outside of your body, and then
objectively observing yourself in action. Let's illustrate
Weisinger's strategies for increasing self-awareness by
using the previous example of the canceled project:

Strategy #1: *Examine how you make judgments about the
world.* Your judgments about yourself, other people,
and situations are influenced by your personality, beliefs, and experiences. By becoming aware of your judgments, you learn how your thoughts influence your
feelings, actions, and reactions, and you can then alter
them accordingly.

> **Positive Reaction:** "My boss canceled my
> project because our funds to pay the vendor
> were cut off. The decision had nothing to do
> with my work."

Remember that it's your own judgments—not someone else's behavior or an external event—that cause your
emotional reactions. You are affected by the meaning that

you assign to events or people you encounter—not the events or people themselves. If you recognize that you tend to put a negative spin on your judgments, remember not to react out of anger, and try and talk yourself out of them.

Strategy #2: *Get in touch with your feelings.* When you understand and acknowledge your emotions, you are better equipped to work through them. You can identify your feelings by being on the lookout for physical manifestations such as increases in heart rate, breathing, and perspiration.

> **Positive Reaction:** "The second the words were out of my boss's mouth, I noticed my heart was beating so fast it was almost in my throat. I didn't need to start talking to know I was really angry."

Strategy #3: *Learn what your intentions are.* Take the time to consider your *hidden agenda*, or what's really driving you to act a certain way, so that you can better strategize your course of action.

> **Positive Reaction:** "I really want to get promoted at my next review, but I'm worried that I won't be able to build a case in time because my primary project was canceled. Maybe I should think about how I can prove myself some other way."

Strategy #4: *Pay attention to your actions.* Nonverbal cues such as speech patterns and body language can clue you in to your emotions and behavior. Becoming aware of these also helps you monitor how others might perceive you.

> **Positive Reaction:** "I can tell I'm feeling really defeated by the way I'm slumping down in my chair. To my boss, it might look as though

I've totally given up on my job because this project was canceled."

● ● ●

By using these self-awareness strategies, you'll be able to better understand your emotional hot buttons and, therefore, manage your negative emotions much more easily. Now, let's introduce some specific tools for diffusing anger, worry, and stress.

Managing Anger

Frustrating circumstances often lead to feelings of anger—that's human nature. However, for the sake of your corporate persona, it's in your best interest to refrain from showing anger at work. Even if you have a legitimate cause, this type of negative reaction will never reflect well on you. Whether you display your anger in the form of an irate tirade, a single rude comment, or subtle insubordination, failing to control this emotion can result in serious consequences. One friend of mine was fired on the spot when he screamed at his boss for handling a project ineptly. Another was suspended from work after sending a scathing e-mail to a colleague. During the most stressful phase of my career, my anger masked itself as tears. I wasn't fired or suspended, but I did compromise my credibility and reputation. All it took was one supervisor to perceive me as immature, and, next thing I knew, I wasn't getting the promotion I deserved.

Regulating your thoughts, existing in the moment, and boosting your EQ are good strategies for preventing negative emotions from creeping into your workday. Despite your best efforts, though, anger may threaten to overflow at times. The key is to manage it so that you don't end up in hot water. In the midst of a heated discussion or situation, use the self-awareness strategies from the last section to determine when you're losing control. Tell the person or people you're arguing with that you need to take a break, and then temporarily remove yourself from the situation. Whether you're right or not is irrelevant. After all, winning the argument won't mean anything if you lose your temper. A month from now, your point will have been forgotten, but everyone who was within earshot will still remember your inappropriate behavior. Go back to your office or cube and decompress. Make an effort to relax, calm yourself down, and adjust your thoughts to erode some of your negativity. Consider ways to reapproach the situation anger-free, and then catch up with your colleague or colleagues to continue the discussion in a civil manner.

Sometimes we need to express our anger physically. This is fine, provided you don't destroy any company property in the process. I suggest taking a time-out and heading outside the building where no one can see you. Wrap an item of clothing around your mouth and scream as loud as you can. It works for me!

Managing Worry

One day last winter, things just weren't going my way. I'm not crazy about my job to begin with, and, on this particular day, my computer wasn't working. I was also managing a major project that was going horribly. I was totally freaking out, so I went to the cafeteria and ran into one of my coworkers. I told him how I was feeling and he said, 'What's the worst thing that could happen?' My response was, 'I could get fired and have to go on welfare.' He went on to ask me if there was much of a chance of that happening. I felt a little silly, but from that point on I refused to let work stress me out too much. Whenever I feel anger or worry starting to overwhelm me, I always think of that conversation.

Kim, 23, Minnesota

Once upon a time, I spent huge amounts of time worrying about the past and the future. I worried when something bad happened, and I worried that something bad *was going* to happen. Then, one day, I visited my grandmother in the hospital. After we talked awhile about my anxiety, my grandmother told me that I was wasting energy, because most of the things we worry about never come to pass. I decided to do a little experiment. I went home and wrote down all of the things I was worried about. A month later, I looked at the list and laughed. The worrisome things that had occurred were already just innocuous memories, and most of the other things had never happened. My grandmother was right. I was wrecking my mental and physical health for virtually no reason at all!

As I've talked about, you can only control the moment you're in right now. Because you can't change the past and you don't know what the future holds, what's the use of worrying about them? As Robert Louis Stevenson once wrote, "Let's be content to live the only time we can possibly live: from now until bedtime. Anyone can carry his burden, however hard, until nightfall." You'd be surprised how negative energy diminishes when you focus solely on the moment at hand. After all, doesn't any problem seem surmountable when you look at it from the vantage point of taking one small step at a time? Now don't get me wrong: You should absolutely prepare for your future as best you can. But once you've done everything possible to increase the likelihood of a positive outcome, let go of your anxiety.

One summer, I worried obsessively about landing an agent to represent my new novel. Every day as I drove home during my lunch break to check the mailbox for agent responses, my blood pressure zoomed into the stratosphere. Several weeks later, I finally recognized that my worry was out of control, and I talked about it with my husband, who is also a psychologist. He said that I should consider the worst-case scenario and resign myself to accepting that outcome if necessary. I took his advice and imagined that I couldn't find an agent, and that my novel would never be published. I then brainstormed ways to improve the situation. This was a hard pill to swallow at first, but I actually felt better once my mind was purged of all the what-ifs? Free from worry, I was able to concentrate rationally on new strategies for obtaining an agent.

Just because you refuse to worry about a problem doesn't mean you are denying its existence. I'm just suggesting that you skip the part where you play out a thousand variations of the same drama in your head. As soon as you become aware of a problem, consider the best way to approach the issue rationally. Make a careful decision based on facts, take action, and then consider the matter over and done with.

There are always going to be bumps in the road, and if you think about it, there's no end to the things you *could* worry about. Remember, though, that those who break the habit of worrying live happier, longer lives. From a practical perspective, they're more productive because they spend time resolving issues rather than fretting over them. They're also more pleasant to be around because they're not constantly surrounded by a cloud of negativity. When you consider all of these benefits, why wouldn't you want to stop worrying?

Managing Stress

The World Health Organization calls job stress a worldwide epidemic. It costs companies billions annually—and what does it cost you? During the first few years of my career in corporate business, I was so stressed that I came home from work every evening and collapsed on the couch. By the time I woke up, it was almost time to go to bed again and I had missed the whole evening. I was in the doctor's office so much with aches and pains and coughs and colds that the nurses thought I was a hypochondriac. I cursed my poor health all the time until I signed up for a self-improvement class. It wasn't until then that I was finally able to put the responsibility where it belonged. There was nothing wrong with my health, but my stress management did need some serious work.

Did you know that people get physically tired because of emotional factors such as boredom, frustration, and anxiety? True intellectual stimulation, on the other hand, doesn't exhaust us at all. If you are drained at the end of the day, it's not because of the mental work you have done, but rather the way in which you did it. The first time I heard this, a lightbulb went off. It occurred to me that I could write nonstop for 8 hours and then run a 5K immediately afterwards, yet after spending a few hours at my corporate job I could barely drag myself to the train station. I now make reducing stress a priority, and I do not consider a day productive unless I have a substantial amount of energy left at the end of it. Here are some strategies for managing stress on a daily basis:

- Identify what stresses you, and plan to cope with it in advance.
- Work in a comfortable position.
- Schedule frequent, short breaks throughout the day.
- Take time-outs to stretch, massage your temples, or get a drink of water.
- Join a gym and go during your lunch break.
- Pick your battles: If it's not worth it, let it go.

There's also no substitute for leading a balanced life. Even if you love your job, remember that people who work all the time are boring, one-dimensional, and, ultimately, unsatisfied. Careers in the corporate world are demanding, but don't let your intellectual, social, and spiritual needs slip through the cracks. Do family members or your old college friends live nearby? Visit them. Do you like to read for pleasure? Pick up that classic novel instead of another industry trade magazine. Spend a few hours volunteering on the weekends, because we feel better when we attempt to make our world better. And regardless of your religion, don't forget to pray. Seriously. Did you know it's been proven that people who practice religion lead more contented lives? They have faith in a power greater than themselves, and their attitudes reflect it.

Three years ago, my roommates made fun of me for sleeping more hours than the average 2 year old. Now my husband has to coax me to bed at midnight. Was my corporate job *then* any harder than it is *now*? Definitely not. In fact, I've climbed the ladder a bit, so my current position is objectively more taxing. The difference now is that

I remind myself every day how stress once destroyed my health and well-being—and I don't let it win!

Motivating Yourself

Whenever I start hating my job, I take on more work so I don't have time to think about it. I find that the busier I am, the less opportunity I have to consider how my company is ruining my career. Because you know what the worst feeling is? Staring at the computer screen, your mind so numb that you can't even think of an Internet site to surf. It's at that moment that every second of the workday feels like an eternity and all of the negative emotions—dissatisfaction, frustration, depression—come flooding in.

Robyn, 25, Nevada

Maintaining a positive attitude is much easier when you're inspired by your work and the people around you. Unfortunately, corporate business today is often not the most motivating environment. Many managers feel that their employees should consider themselves lucky to have jobs, and they see no reason to lead and encourage them. Twenty-somethings find themselves working more hours, while rewards and recognition for stellar performance are few and far between. Not to mention, channels of career progression are more confusing than ever. Considering these circumstances, who could blame you for going into work every day and doing the bare minimum? The corporate establishment doesn't deserve anything more.

The problem is, having an attitude like that only hurts you. Here's why: If you're playing your cards right, you're using your job as the means for achieving your big-picture career objectives. Therefore, when you stop giving your all because you didn't get a raise or someone didn't pat you on the back for a job well done, you're sabotaging your own goals. Meeting your own criteria for success should be motivation enough, don't you think?

Getting motivated is not as simple as it sounds when it's a rainy Monday morning, an angry client is on the phone, and you have urgent deadlines to meet. You can use this chapter's strategies to give your attitude a boost, but don't underestimate the importance of firing yourself up to do your best every day. Need a crutch? I suggest rereading a cheesy self-help book of your choice and posting some of your favorite inspirational quotes in your cube or office. Share your motivational tips with others, and you'll be surprised how much easier it is to believe in them yourself. Sign up for any personal development or leadership courses your company offers, and stay busy so you don't have time to sit around and think about how much better your job situation could be.

Always keep the big picture in the forefront of your mind, but don't forget to acknowledge your little successes along the way. Every time you master a new skill or finish a tough project, celebrate the fact that you're one step closer to your overall career goal. And just because your corporate colleagues don't give you kudos doesn't mean your friends and family won't. Tell them!

No matter how hard you try to rally against negativity, there are going to be times when you feel like marching straight over to your boss's office and handing in your resignation.

Beating yourself up for feeling this way will only upset you more. Instead, be patient and wait for the mood to pass. You might also try this suggestion from Hendrie Weisinger, author of *Emotional Intelligence at Work*: Pretend it's your first day of a new job, and imagine approaching every task with confidence, eagerness, and enthusiasm. You can do the same thing by imagining that this is the best day of your working life. You are full of energy and ideas, you're getting lots of things accomplished, and people are responding to you with praise. Maybe it will be a self-fulfilling prophecy!

Damage Control

In an ideal world, you would never cop an attitude with one of your colleagues or managers. Given that you're human, though, this is an unrealistic expectation. Sometimes you will take your aggravation out on another person whether she deserves it or not. Provided you have a good rapport with your coworker and handle yourself correctly, one incident should not permanently affect the relationship (see Chapter 7).

When you lose your cool, you might feel embarrassed and want to pretend the incident never happened. This is not a good strategy. If you go too long without addressing the issue, the person you've offended might build up the interaction in her mind to be worse than it actually was, and she will remember it the next time the two of you talk. Before you know it, you'll have established a pattern of negative communication.

Effective damage control means taking responsibility for your actions. If you clash with a colleague, honestly assess the situation and look at it from the other person's viewpoint. Remember that being right doesn't justify rudeness or inappropriate behavior. Let go of your pride. It takes guts to go back and make it right, and your colleague will respect you for it. Approach the person and sincerely apologize for your role in the altercation. Explain that you're still learning, and assure her it won't happen again. Can't stomach an in-person conversation? Write a heartfelt letter or e-mail instead. Your colleague will likely be receptive to the overture. Instead of thinking you're a jerk, she will now perceive you as being mature beyond your years. Just another example of how a little effort on your part can turn most negative situations into positive ones!

Chapter 6 Take Home Points

✓ **Choose a positive outlook.** Your thoughts make you who you are. You are responsible for your own life, and you have the ability to choose your response to your environment. If you make a conscious decision to begin each day with a positive outlook, negative conditions at work can't take that away from you.

✓ **Increase your self-awareness.** Begin to better understand your emotional hot buttons. Examine how you make judgments about the world, tune in to your senses, get in touch with your feelings, learn what your intentions are, and pay attention to your actions.

✓ **Imagine the worst-case scenario.** When you imagine the worst-case scenario and reconcile yourself to accepting that outcome if necessary, you stop worry in its tracks. Then, you will be able to rationally focus on ways to improve the situation.

✓ **Motivate yourself on a daily basis.** Motivate yourself by striving to meet your own criteria for success. Instead of relying on external validation, focus on using your job as the means for achieving your big-picture career objectives.

Chapter 7

People Management

One company I worked for offered a course designed to improve employees' interpersonal skills. I was in public relations and interacted with people all the time, so it was a no-brainer for me to sign up. On the first day of class, I was surprised to see that I was the only marketing person in the group. Most of my classmates were computer programmers and graphic designers. Later, I asked one of the programming supervisors why he wanted his people to take this class. After all, these folks sat in front of machines all day long—it wasn't unusual for them to go from morning coffee to lunch without talking to a single human being.

"Aren't some folks drawn to programming because they don't want to deal with people, because the interpersonal stuff makes them uncomfortable?" I asked.

"That's sometimes true," the supervisor said. "And it's all the more reason for them to take this class. There's no such thing as a job that doesn't require people skills. My staff might talk to a customer or colleague only once a day, but if that interaction goes badly, it will snowball, and I just can't afford that."

Let this be a lesson for all of us. Throughout this book I've talked about how being the best and the brightest won't get you very far in corporate business if you can't communicate effectively with the people around you. An individual who has mastered the art of people management gets things accomplished by leveraging his efforts in concert with the efforts of others. This is not always easy to do. How many times have we said to ourselves, "If only I didn't need to rely on Person A and could do Task X by myself, everything would be just peachy." Well, in this chapter I'll cover strategies for enlisting your colleagues' cooperation so that you can increase the control you have over your own success. We'll also spend some time on the underrated concept of gratitude in the workplace, as well as examine strategies for creating positive relationships and coping with difficult personalities.

Enlisting Cooperation

Last year I graduated from college and took a job in a medium-size life insurance firm. I had always considered myself pretty levelheaded, but I just couldn't figure out how to get along in the work world. I felt like my future at the company depended on the actions of other people, so every time I tried to get a colleague to do something, it was like going into the boxing ring. It turned into a vicious cycle. The more I tried to force things on people, the more I alienated them. Then they were angry, I was angry, no one got anything done, and the tension in the office became so great that someone had to go. Guess who was the lucky loser?

John, 24, Pennsylvania

During my tenure in the corporate world, I've seen people try all sorts of tactics, from bribery to temper tantrums, to get others to do what they want. Some use their power or position to force lower-ranking staff to comply. In today's fast-paced business culture, many middle managers are too harried and apathetic to stop and consider the best way to encourage true cooperation. In his book *The 7 Habits of Highly Effective People*, Stephen Covey outlines a number of approaches that individuals use when trying to get something from another person. Covey catagorizes these approaches as Win/Win, Win/Lose, Lose/Win, Lose/Lose, and Win. Let me further explain:

- **Win/Win** *(I call this the "Barney" approach—"I love you, you love me")*: The attitude that a mutually beneficial solution is the best solution because everyone feels good and one person's success is not achieved at the expense of another.

- **Win/Lose** *(I call this the "competitive" approach—"I get my way, you don't get yours")*: The attitude that someone else has to lose in order for you to win, like in football games and lawsuits.

- **Lose/Win** *(I call this the "wuss" approach—"Go ahead, have your way with me. Everyone else does")*: The attitude of people who are quick to please or appease, repressing their true feelings and seeking strength from popularity or acceptance.

- **Lose/Lose** *(I call this the "Mexican standoff" approach—"I'm going to win or die trying")*: The thinking that results when two Win/Lose people become stubborn, vindictive, and blind to everything except their desire for the other person to lose.

- **Win** *(I call this the "shrugged shoulders" approach—"Do what you need to do, I can't be bothered")*: The attitude that it doesn't matter whether the other person wins or loses, as long as you get what you want.

It's easy to fall into the trap of thinking that every interaction in the cutthroat world of corporate business has to be Win/Lose. But because you work with the same colleagues every day, this attitude (and the manipulation and coercion tactics that often go with it) can cost you big time. Before you know it, your work relationships will have soured, and your corporate persona will be seriously tarnished. In most cases, you'll be more effective at eliciting your colleagues' cooperation and, ultimately, getting what you want if you make Win/Win your personal philosophy.

Win/Win outcomes are easier to achieve when you proactively consider ways that the other person can benefit from cooperating with you. That said, one of the biggest mistakes you can make is to enter a negotiation by expressly stating what you want. You might have heard the story of the salesman who greets a prospect by announcing, "I want to tell you about a great new product that has a thousand new features, all for the low price of..." The prospect stops listening as soon as she hears the words *I want* and slams the door in the salesman's face. If you're going to remember anything from this section, remember this: Other people don't care what you want. They want to know what's in it for them. As the initiator of a negotiation, you have to assume that while you may be looking for the Win/Win, the other person is interested only in the Win. Need her cooperation? Make her *want* to do what you are asking.

How do you do this? First, examine the situation from her point of view and determine her priorities. Then, in your initial approach, talk about what she wants and how your proposal can help her get it. Here's an example of this strategy in action: My job is to coordinate press interviews between executives and journalists. A few weeks ago, I had to persuade a high-level sales executive to postpone a visit with a client and spend an hour talking with a journalist on deadline. However, I understood that the sales executive wanted to spend his time closing deals, not chatting it up with someone who couldn't pay him. So I approached my request this way:

"You mentioned that we sometimes lose deals because we can't demonstrate to potential clients how our products are covered in the press. Here is our chance to change that. Ordinarily I wouldn't ask you to move your meeting, but the client is available for lunch on Friday. The article with your interview will have appeared by then—why don't I get you a copy to show him?"

In this way, the sales executive saw how talking with the journalist could help him get what he wanted: more closed deals. He realized that spending an hour *now* would pay huge publicity dividends later on, and that it might even help persuade the client he planned on visiting that week. I got my interview done on time, and the sales executive met the client for lunch armed with an extra weapon. Win/Win!

It doesn't matter if the other person *actually* wins by cooperating with you, as long as she *feels* like she's winning. For instance, you can frequently achieve a positive outcome by appealing to a person's moral code. In his book *How to Win Friends and Influence People*, motivational guru Dale Carnegie claims that people like to feel as though they are doing the proper, unselfish thing. If your proposal will make the other person feel good about herself, she'll be more inclined to cooperate. To take the example above one step further, suppose the sales executive needed a bit more convincing to change his schedule and meet with the journalist. I could have played to his desire to do what's best for the company with the following response:

"Our company has gotten some undeservedly negative press lately, and we're lucky to be in a position to counter it with some positive messages of our own. When unflattering articles appear, our stock goes down. But when spokespeople like you get out there and talk with the media about the good things we're doing, the reverse happens!"

Bottom line, Win/Win scenarios are usually within reach when you take the time to think about what you're asking of someone and how you're going to ask it. Imagine yourself in the other person's position and treat her as you would want to be treated under the same circumstances. Keeping in mind that the end goal is cooperation, remove your ego from the situation and don't insist that people do things your way. Your colleagues will be more likely to pursue a project if they have a say in how it's done, so instead of bullying them into following your lead, outline what you need and ask for feedback on the best way to accomplish it. After all, if the work gets done and everyone is happy about it, it's a Win/Win regardless of how you arrived there.

A Touch of Sweetness

So many of the senior executives in my agency treat underlings like dirt. We are expected to bend over backwards for them without so much as a 'thank you.' One manager, however, is noticeably different. This person doesn't take for granted that we'll do whatever he says because he has the power to fire us. He's great about complimenting us for a job well done, which, in turn, motivates us to do even better for him in the future. I observed this exec for a while and noticed that no one ever seemed to praise him for being such a good manager. So, one day, I did. I told him that I didn't want him to think I was kissing up, but that I thought he deserved to know that I appreciated his efforts. You should have seen him light up—it was like my comment was the best thing that happened to him all week.

Sabrinath, 23, New Mexico

Imagine the look on a colleague's face when you hand over a tasty piece of candy unsolicited. Appreciation is the same way. You only need a little bit to make a coworker's day and encourage her to view you in a positive light from that point on. Did someone help you out? Thank her. Was it a big deal, did she go out of her way, or did it take a lot of time? Send her a card or flowers, or take her to lunch. If she really went above and beyond the call of duty, make sure her boss knows about it. And by the way, I don't subscribe to the theory that you shouldn't have to thank someone for doing her job. When a colleague does her job well and it helps you, what harm does it do to thank her? The answer is none—it just makes her like you more.

Eighteenth-century author Samuel Johnson wrote, "Gratitude is a fruit of great cultivation; you do not find it among gross people." Well, folks, times haven't changed. Most people still take good deeds and favors for granted, and you're bound to be disappointed if you do something nice and expect appreciation in return. Instead of demanding gratitude, give freely. Exhibit kindness, and go out of your way to show courtesy and consideration to each person you come in contact with. Answer your phone ready and willing to accommodate the person on the other end. Ask how you can help, listen to the answer, and then follow up quickly and cheerfully.

As we've talked about, it doesn't make sense to reserve your best behavior for your customers and your boss, because when it comes to your reputation, everyone is equally influential. Remember that people have big mouths that get even bigger when they're unhappy. All it takes is one person to complain that you were rude or uncooperative, and, next thing you know, everyone in the office will have the scoop.

People hunger for recognition. In fact, their happiness, self-esteem, and motivation depend on it. Be generous with your compliments, but make sure they're sincere. Empty flattery is, in many ways, worse than criticism. Don't praise every move someone makes, and when you do give a compliment, put substance behind the statement so it's meaningful to the person. The most effective compliments focus on specific actions or facts rather than vague generalities or assumptions. Here are a couple examples:

> **Weak Compliment:** "You did a great job on that presentation."
> **Strong Compliment:** "The analogies you made in your presentation really engaged the audience members because they could relate what you were saying to their own lives."

> **Weak Compliment:** "You're so organized."
> **Strong Compliment:** "You were so prepared in that customer meeting. I appreciated the way

you had supporting information to back up each of our claims."

When you receive a compliment, don't downplay or dismiss it. This makes you look insecure, and it makes the other person feel uncomfortable and stupid. You don't always have to return the compliment either. A smile and a simple "thank you" will do. If you're concerned about modesty, share the credit with someone else.

While we're on the subject of credit, always acknowledge people's achievements—both large and small. You don't appreciate when your own success is met with silence, and others don't either. And in case this wasn't obvious already, make a point of calling attention to the things people do right, not just what they do wrong. Your colleagues will be more receptive to your ideas when they don't have to brace themselves for criticism every time you open your mouth.

Sharing appreciation and praise helps those of us who lean naturally toward the "glass half empty" mentality to focus on the finer aspects of other people and their behavior. Not only does this behavior strengthen our relationships and encourage cooperation, but it also positively impacts the way we think about ourselves and the world.

Creating Positive Relationships

My expectations for myself are pretty high, and the biggest mistake I made during my first year as a manager was imposing those same expectations on the person who worked for me. This girl was very different from me. While she still

managed to get her work done on time, she was
not nearly as organized or efficient about it as I
am. I was frustrated with her and showed it pretty
often. I even held back her promotion because
she hadn't mastered, overnight, skills that come
naturally to me. Nearly in tears, she told me she
felt like she could never please me. Looking back,
she was probably right.

Marissa, 26, Ottawa

When it comes to relationship building, corporate business diverges sharply from the educational experiences of
childhood and adolescence. As I've already discussed,
achievement is an individual endeavor in grade school
through college. Even if you didn't have a good teacher or
friends to help you with your homework, you could still
master the material on your own and get an A. Like it or
not, the business world is a different animal. You need
other people to get ahead, and each interpersonal relationship you create has the potential to do more for your
career than reading 100 books about your trade.

Most of us develop relationships every day without even
thinking about it. Sometimes we select the people we want
to associate with based on common interests, lifestyles, and
personality traits. Other times we fall into relationships because they are convenient at a particular point in time (for
example, neighbor-to-neighbor). Work relationships are
similar to family relationships. We don't necessarily choose
them and we might prefer not to have them, but, for our
sanity's sake, we have to make them work as best we can.

Because they don't come as naturally, work relationships can be difficult to care for and maintain if you're not

paying attention. In his book *The 7 Habits of Highly Effective People*, Stephen Covey introduces the concept of the "emotional bank account" to help us consciously manage our most constant relationships. In every emotional bank account, we save trust and goodwill through deposits of kindness, honesty, and keeping our word. When the reserve of trust in an account is high, communication is instant, easy, and effective. On the other hand, if we continually show another person disrespect, the trust account diminishes, and the slightest provocation can turn into a relationship "incident." In other words, having an ongoing positive rapport with someone means that he will give you a break when you make a mistake.

Here's an example of the emotional bank account in action. I have a strong, mutually beneficial relationship with my colleague Michelle. One afternoon, I had to meet with a client even though I wasn't feeling well. During the meeting, Michelle justifiably asked me a question, and I bit her head off. If Michelle and I didn't have such a good relationship, she might have been offended by my rudeness. However, when I apologized to her later, I found that she had already forgotten it. "I didn't take it personally," Michelle said. "I knew it wasn't like you and that something must be going on." Fortunately, Michelle and I had enough trust built up to cover the withdrawal to our emotional bank account. I also made an additional deposit when I apologized for my bad behavior.

Whether you make a withdrawal or not, your account reserves need constant replenishing. Old deposits evaporate with time, so a person isn't necessarily going to remember a favor you did for him months ago if the two of you haven't had another positive interaction since then. As I mentioned in the previous section, showing appreciation, praising superior work, and complimenting when appropriate are great techniques for keeping your relationships healthy and productive. Here are a few more ways you can make routine deposits to your emotional bank accounts:

- Take a sincere interest in the other person and what's meaningful to him.
- Attend to the little things, such as returning a phone call or acknowledging his birthday.
- Deliver on anything and everything you promise.
- Make a concerted effort to keep the lines of communication open.
- Remember his name and the names of the important people in his life.
- Demonstrate integrity under all circumstances.

You can also improve your relationships by effectively managing your expectations of other people. Remember those evil *shoulds* from Chapter 6? Author and psychologist Hendrie Weisinger warns against expecting too much from your relationships. Consciously or unconsciously, you may want your boss to be in a good mood all of the time or your admin to be as pathologically detail-oriented as you are. However, when your expectations exceed what other people *can* or *will* do, you become frustrated and disappointed. You can prevent your relationships from taking a beating by ensuring that your expectations are reasonable and realistic. If you're not sure, seek advice from a mentor or trusted colleague who has been in your position before. Once you've clarified your expectations in your own mind, make certain you accurately communicate them to the other person. Solicit feedback in advance so that you can uncover potential roadblocks and avoid being caught off guard later on.

Being Mentally Present

> I hate it when my coworker suggests lunch meetings in the cafeteria, because, inevitably, the two of us will be sitting there together and he'll start looking past me at everything going on and everyone around us. I know the caf's a happening place, but come on! Whatever happened to listening and making eye contact? Sometimes I wonder if he would even notice if I stopped talking. It's downright embarrassing.
>
> Heather, 25, Georgia

Want to know an important yet significantly underrated strategy for building strong workplace relationships? Simply make a habit of being present for every person you deal with— not just *physically* present, mind you, but *mentally* present. This means actually listening to what the other person is saying, focusing on him rather than everything else going on in the room, and ignoring potential interruptions, such as ringing phones or e-mails that pop into your inbox.

When someone comes to your office or cube, decide right then and there if you have time to talk. If you don't, say so. If you do have time, but only a little bit, ask them if it's enough. You don't necessarily have to drop everything for the person, but once you make the commitment to have a dialogue, please be respectful. Remember that his time is important too, and give him your full attention. Doing this will set you apart from the scores of corporate employees who believe that sitting across the desk from another person means you're communicating.

Several years ago I had a boss who took every call and read every new e-mail that came in while I was meeting with her. She was a great manager otherwise, but I get a bad taste in my mouth when I think of how every meeting took a half hour instead of 5 minutes because she prioritized every interruption ahead of me. I shall now retire my soapbox, but you get the point. Don't become one of them! Try to be mentally present for every person you talk to, every day.

Dealing With Difficult People

At some point in our careers, most of us are forced to work with someone whose people skills can only be described as atrocious. Sometimes our companies wisely get rid of these people, but they are like weeds: Pluck one, and within seconds another will sprout up in its place. The dread that comes with having to regularly interact with someone who is routinely negative, argumentative, stressed, or mean can make your job a wholly unpleasant experience—if you let it.

Your first instinct might be to go out of your way to avoid working with "Mr. Difficult." If you can pull it off, more power to you. Often, though, this is not an option, and whether Mr. Difficult is your boss, a colleague, or a senior executive, you must prepare for each meeting with him as if you are going into battle. Swallow your apprehension. Remind yourself that no one has the power to control how you feel, and suit up in your armor so that nothing he says or does wounds you deeply. Take a deep breath and walk calmly into Mr. Difficult's office. Speak to him in a controlled, cheerful, and reasonable tone. Get the information you need, and then get out as soon as possible. As we know, negativity and stress can be highly contagious, so do not allow yourself to get sucked in.

Mr. Difficult's arrows can be easier to deflect when he's an equal opportunity shooter, and you realize that you are not the only target. You might even joke about him with your other colleagues who have had the pleasure to work with him directly. However, it's easy to become demoralized when Mr. Difficult saves his best poison just for you. For example, one of my first bosses couldn't stand me. To the best of my knowledge, I didn't do anything to incur her wrath. She was sweet as apple pie to the rest of our colleagues, yet, inexplicably, whenever I came around, she turned into the Wicked Witch of the West. Unfortunately, this is not unusual in corporate business. Personality clashes often happen. Your best bet in this scenario is to sit down with your Mr. Difficult and have a heart-to-heart. Tell him how you are feeling, assume that he doesn't mean to act like the devil incarnate, and give him the benefit of the doubt. Solicit his feedback regarding how the two of you can improve your relationship, and then give him a chance to do right by you. If this doesn't work and he continues to regularly use you as target practice, remove yourself from the situation (see Chapter 10). No job is worth your self-esteem.

One caveat to all of this: Human beings operate with such different styles that it's impossible for us to get along with all of our colleagues all of the time. You could be the most agreeable person on earth, but I guarantee that someone at work will find a reason not to like you. Maybe she isn't blatantly obvious or malicious like Mr. Difficult, but you can feel her negativity just the same. She might walk right past your desk without saying good morning, or she might not engage in friendly conversation with you the way she does with other people in the office. For those of us with a sensitive streak, this type of behavior can be hurtful.

What did you do to her anyway? Why won't she give you a fair shot? As natural as it is to fixate on the situation, if it's not affecting your daily work life or your career path, refuse to take it personally, and go about your business as usual. Focus on your reasons for being at work, and save your energy for the people in the office who deserve it.

Criticism Incoming

The sun rises in the morning, and human beings criticize each other. Stick around the corporate world for a while, and you will inevitably participate in this special ritual. What separates the strong employees from the weak, however, is how one copes with criticism. People who deny responsibility and respond with anger and defensiveness hold themselves back personally and professionally. On the other hand, the most successful individuals listen objectively, accept constructive criticism, and look for ways to grow from it. In his book *Getting Promoted: Real Strategies for Advancing Your Career*, Harry Chambers suggests the following five steps for receiving criticism productively:

1. **Depersonalize the criticism:** *Repeat to yourself*, "It's a specific behavior that's the problem, not me as a person."

2. **Assertively restate the comments for clarification:** *Say to the person*, "What I heard was that this behavior is not acceptable."

3. **Seek guidance:** *Ask the person*, "How could I do that differently? What change would be appropriate?"

4. **Process the input:** *Ask yourself*, "Is this criticism valid? Am I willing to make the change to eliminate the contention?"

5. **Review your progress/seek follow-up:** *Say to the person*, "I'm working hard to bring about

the change we talked about. Do you have any suggestions for what else I can do?"

Provided the criticism is meant to help you, be sensitive to what the other person is feeling. It was probably very difficult for her to approach you, and you will score major points by trying to make her more comfortable. Also, there's nothing wrong with telling her how you feel. If the criticism isn't justified, say so frankly, without letting your emotions get the best of you.

One last point on criticism: Eleanor Roosevelt once said, "Do what you feel in your heart to be right—for you'll be criticized anyway." Keep in mind that if you are accomplishing something, you will most likely be criticized by someone who secretly wishes that she were as important as you are. Take it as a compliment, for it means you are worthy of attention.

Calming an Angry Person

Customer service representatives have to contend with angry people frequently, and my friend Jan, who spends all day on the telephone, offered me some valuable advice for neutralizing someone who is out of control. According to Jan, the best thing you can do is acknowledge the person's anger and listen attentively without interrupting. "If you let the customer vent, she'll eventually quiet down," Jan says. "Don't respond with defensiveness or annoyance. Show empathy for her predicament and assure her that you'll make it your business to fix the situation." Jan also clued me in on some things *not* to say:

- *"Calm down"*: This is bound to elicit the response, "Don't tell me to calm down!"
- *"That's not my fault"*: Whether true or not, the angry person will not appreciate hearing you deny responsibility. She is looking for *your* help.

- *"You're way out of line"*: Needless to say, this will just prolong the argument.
- *"If you just hold on, I'll transfer you to…"*: This lack of urgency and personal ownership will annoy the angry person. She wants you to come up with an action plan now.

"The key point," Jan says, "is to remain calm. If the customer is not able to engage you in an argument, she'll eventually stop fighting. People can't be pissed off by themselves for long. Your calmness will diffuse her anger, and then the two of you can work together to solve the problem."

Chapter 7 Take Home Points

✓ **Choose a Win/Win attitude.** Other people don't care what you want—they want to know what's in it for them. By approaching negotiations with a Win/Win attitude, you'll be more effective at eliciting cooperation and, ultimately, getting what you want.

✓ **Compliment your coworkers.** People hunger for recognition. Be generous with your compliments, but make sure they're sincere. The most effective compliments focus on specific actions or facts rather than vague generalities or assumptions.

✓ **Give coworkers your undivided attention.** Being mentally present for another person means actually listening to what she is saying, focusing on her rather than everything else going on in the room, and ignoring potential interruptions, such as ringing phones or new e-mails.

✓ **Lean to handle criticism with class.** The most successful people in corporate business listen objectively, accept constructive criticism, and look for ways to grow from it. Those who respond to criticism by getting defensive hold themselves back personally and professionally.

Chapter 8

Moving Up in the World

There may be no greater challenge in corporate business than getting promoted. For every factor you can control (such as your skills and abilities), there are at least two that you can't (such as the economy and your company's infrastructure). Career author Harry Chambers tells us that in the era of streamlined organizations, companies have been flattened and downsized so that there are fewer middle-management positions for twenty-somethings to be promoted into. Also, a "do more with less" mentality often translates into increases in responsibilities without additional compensation or acknowledgment.

For some, a job in the corporate world is just a pit stop on the way to a career in another field—such as entertainment. These individuals might define success as a check that pays for their true passion rather than a promotion that moves them to the next level. Unfortunately, there are many more twenty-somethings struggling to build careers in corporate business, and, as such, competition for promotion opportunities has become so intense that doing all of the right things might not necessarily get you the recognition you deserve.

If you're in the latter category, giving up is not an option. You have no choice but to ensure your promotability. If you don't move ahead now while you're young and unencumbered, you may never manage it at all. Instead, you could end up stuck at or near the bottom rung with bosses who are younger and less experienced than you. Also, your resume will look suspicious to potential new employers.

The good news is that you are much more likely to be promoted in your 20s, because, as a newbie, the whole world is open to you, and you have nowhere to go but up. Everything I've discussed in this book so far—from setting and achieving goals, to maintaining strong communication and interpersonal skills—will better your chances of landing a promotion. In this chapter I'll drill down a little deeper into strategies that will help you grab hold of that ever-elusive brass ring. I'll also talk about how to troubleshoot an antipromotion situation, and also how to cope when your quest for reward and recognition takes an unfavorable turn.

Acing Performance Reviews

Every time I sit down for a review with my boss, I feel like a deer caught in the headlights. Talking about myself makes me incredibly uncomfortable, so I can go the whole hour without saying a word. My boss will ramble on and on, and I'll just sit there and nod dumbly like an idiot. When he's done, he'll push the review in front of me and ask me to sign it. I'll do it, no questions asked, but as soon as I leave the room, I'll think of 20

> things I should have gotten off my chest before
> signing that paper. By then, though, it's too late.
>
> Debbie, 23, Texas

Most people roll their eyes when it comes time for performance reviews. This is because the review is, by nature, an uncomfortable and contrived process. In most companies, reviews happen once or twice a year, and, during this time, every employee is forced to sit in a room with his boss and talk turkey about how he's progressed and how he's screwed up. Performance review documentation is notorious for being generic and vague, complete with ratings that are totally subjective and impossible to measure. Unfortunately, many reviews also take place in a vacuum: The items discussed are often not mentioned again until the next review. Twenty-somethings may perceive reviews as yet another bureaucratic exercise that wastes valuable time and need not be taken seriously. However, for all its flaws, the performance review is the only door to promotion inside much of the business world, so you must take advantage of it if you want to get ahead.

If you don't care about your review, no one else will. The worst thing you can do for your career is to go through the process passively. Whether your company's review cycle takes place annually or biannually, your preparation should typically start weeks before. Think of your review as an opportunity to sell your manager on your value to the company. If you've mapped out clear career goals (see Chapter 4), and you and your boss have discussed them on an ongoing basis, you'll have a great head start. Take your last review out of the file cabinet and dust it off. Look at the goals and/or action steps outlined last time around, and gather facts to support how you've progressed in each area. Brainstorm concrete examples that illustrate outstanding performance, and practice communicating them so they're on the tip of your tongue. Then make a list of all the things you would like to cover in the review meeting, independent of your manager's agenda. Your objectives will probably include soliciting feedback on your progress, identifying new goals and growth opportunities, and hammering out a long-term promotion plan. This last item is particularly important. While you can't reasonably expect to be promoted after every review, you should at least leave with an understanding of where your current responsibilities are leading.

When it comes time for the actual review, make sure your boss gives it to you. This may sound ridiculous, but you'd be surprised how many companies will allow managers to get away with skipping the review process entirely. After all, bosses are busy, and employee reviews are not on the top of their list of priorities. Remember, though, that it's your right to request a timely appraisal. During the meeting itself, maintain a good balance between listening to what your manager has to say and playing an active role in the conversation. Just because your boss offers constructive criticism doesn't mean you won't get a promotion or a raise, so keep your defensiveness to a minimum. Even though a casual chitchat session might be more comfortable and fun than a serious conversation about your career aspirations, insist on getting through your objectives for the meeting. To paraphrase career author Harry Chambers, your performance review is your best—if not your only—opportunity to get a clear understanding of how you are perceived and what you need to do to ensure your future success.

Don't be afraid to ask questions about your boss's feedback, and make sure you read over your written review carefully before signing it. Once the cycle is complete, your manager might be perfectly happy to forget about your performance for the next five or 11 months. Don't let her. Be proactive about setting up regular meetings to review your progress, address potential problems, and incorporate new responsibilities and priorities into the master plan. If you keep the lines of communication open, nothing that comes up in your next review will be a surprise. Who knows, maybe you'll even look forward to it!

Asking for a Raise

If you are going to ask your boss for a raise, make sure you have a good reason—and needing the money doesn't count! Your company doesn't care if you are drowning in student loans, can't make your rent, or have to finance a wedding this year. Like everything else in corporate business, the money you get paid is all about the value you add to the company. Before you sit down with your manager, you'll want to be prepared with a list of contributions that have positively impacted the bottom line. As you're putting together your case, be hard on yourself. Look at the situation from your company's point of view. Have you honestly acquired such valuable skills, performed at such a high level, and exceeded expectations to such a degree that your company should shell out more assets to keep you?

You also have to look at the big picture. Check out compensation surveys such as the National Compensation Survey by the U.S. Department of Labor (*www.bls.gov/ncs*) or Websites such as *www.salary.com* to determine how your salary stacks up to what other local twenty-somethings in your position are making. Don't forget to take into account other financial incentives you may receive from your company, including bonuses, stock options, insurance packages, 401(k) contributions, and tuition reimbursement.

Of course, you also have to get real and evaluate your request in the context of the current economic conditions, your company's financial status, and internal policies regarding raises. In today's business climate particularly, many companies are foregoing merit increases or are only issuing them at a certain time of the year. Also, some companies have *grades*, or fixed salary ranges, that prevent managers from increasing compensation beyond the amount predetermined by your level or title. Still, others may place the authority to decide matters of compensation in the hands of a few individuals—and your boss may not be one of them. You'll save yourself a lot of agita if you find out about such things ahead of time.

When is a good time to ask for a raise? Coming off a strong performance review in which your boss acknowledged your accomplishments is a good bet because he will probably be expecting you to broach the subject of money. If you have just taken on a new role or your management has raised the bar for your performance, it is perfectly legitimate to ask for an appointment to discuss "compensation commensurate with new responsibilities."

When scheduling the meeting, pick a time when your boss's stress level and workload are as manageable as possible, and tell him what you want to talk about so that he's prepared. An informal setting such as lunch often works best because it allows you to relate to your manager on a personal level. Before you meet face to face, decide on a number that you'd be satisfied with, and think about how you'll respond if you don't get it. You also may want to practice your tone on a family member or friend prior to the meeting, because there is a fine line separating the assertive/sincere and boastful/arrogant approaches.

Now, on to the big conversation itself. If you're underpaid and you know it, refrain from bitching. Acting bitter or angry will only put your manager on the defensive. Instead, remain calm, positive, and professional. Tell your boss how much you enjoy working for the company. Talk about your performance in a factual manner and provide concrete examples of how you add value to the organization. When it comes time to broach the topic, use the word *compensation* rather than *raise* or *money*. In the event that your boss declines your raise, don't close your ears to the rest of the discussion. He may be willing to offer you other perks instead, such as extra vacation time, flexible hours, or a nice dinner with your significant other on the company. These concessions may not be as valuable as cold cash, but they can come in handy for a twenty-something struggling to afford the good life outside of work.

Despite your best efforts, you may not get the compensation you've earned. This is not an unusual scenario for twenty-somethings in corporate business. In this day and age, the only way to get a serious pay increase is to switch jobs (see Chapter 10). But if you are not willing to switch jobs, try and swallow your negativity at not getting a raise for the time being, ask your boss what you need to do in order to receive an increase, and found out if it's possible to revisit this issue in a few months. Do not give an ultimatum unless you are prepared to walk out the door right then and there. Just remember: Even if you have another job offer in hand that pays more, you cannot assume that your current manager will make a counteroffer.

Your boss may tell you that he would like to give you a raise, but his hands are tied. If this is the case, ask him if the two of you can schedule a meeting with the higher-up responsible for the decision. Do not go over his head without his knowledge, and make sure he is kept in the loop on all matters concerning your compensation.

Raise discussions are never easy for either party, and if your boss is the passive-aggressive type, he may tell you what you want to hear simply to get you out of his office. Make sure that you follow up appropriately on any verbal promises he makes, and, if possible, secure an effective date for your increase. The issue is not closed until you see the change in your paycheck.

Pleasing the Promotion Gods

I wasn't in with the right people at my company, so the good work that I did was constantly overlooked by the higher-ups. I watched kids five or six years younger than me getting all these high-profile assignments, and I started to get burned up about it. So I decided to try a different strategy. I love playing racquetball, so I signed up for the company tournament and just 'happened' to get paired with a senior exec in my division. We got to know each other a lot during that week, and I dropped in just enough info about work so that this guy knew what I was made of. When one of his employees left the company, I asked him if he was looking for a replacement. He hadn't thought about it yet, and he didn't think about it anymore—he hired me!

Mike, 29, New Jersey

In case this wasn't obvious already, you need to do more than just master the performance review process and leave the rest to chance if you want to get promoted. According to Harry Chambers, author of *Getting Promoted: Real Strategies for Advancing Your Career*, factors that affect promotion include:

1. Yourself (your skills, your abilities, and your willingness to do what you need to do in order to get ahead).
2. Your visibility in the organization and people's perceptions of you.
3. Opportunities within the organization to move up the ladder.

Intentionally moving your career in the right direction means successfully controlling Factor #1, influencing Factor #2, and assessing Factor #3.

Chambers suggests that people who want to be promoted do the following:

- Perform at such a high level that their candidacy cannot be denied.
- Demonstrate informal leadership before formal authority is attained.
- Keep themselves free of baggage and political skirmishes.
- Position themselves as agents of change who are willing to support current company policies, while also embracing future opportunities.
- Seek to expand their influence and challenges by broadening the scope of their responsibilities.
- Develop and support the people they work with by driving processes forward.

Of course, the skills I've discussed throughout this book, including maintaining a strong corporate persona, proactively setting goals, confronting and solving problems, communicating effectively, and greeting challenges with a positive attitude will serve you well as you position yourself for your next promotion. I also cannot emphasize enough the importance of relationships in this process. In Chapter 3, I talked about how networking can increase your visibility and establish personal connections that will help you move forward. Reading this book cover to cover and becoming as good an employee as Serena Williams is a tennis player will not do the job unless you get out there and meet the right people. At this stage in your career, you should be jumping at any opportunity to interact with higher-ups—from attending your company's social events and sitting in the right place in the cafeteria, to volunteering to work on special projects and serving on office committees. In these situations, don't be afraid to strut your stuff. Just be sure you know what you're talking about!

It also doesn't hurt to be assertive in determining your own destiny. Just like asking for a raise, bringing up the topic of promotion with your manager is appropriate and legitimate, provided you've earned the right to move to the next level. Rather than accosting your boss in the hall during a moment of extraordinary stress and blurting out, "I want a promotion," give the matter a great deal of thought before initiating a conversation. Develop a bullet-proof case for why you are entitled to advance by making a list of the weekly hours you spend doing tasks inside your job description and the weekly hours you spend doing tasks at the next level. The goal of this little exercise is to show that you are accomplishing much more than you were originally hired to do. If you're doing the work of more than one full-time employee, note that as well. Then, as you're talking to your boss, point out that your efficiency saves him money because he only has to pay one person instead of two.

Be prepared to compromise. No matter how valuable you are, chances are your boss is not going to promote you right then and there, so talk in terms of time frames and how you can ensure that you perform at a level that will warrant a promotion in three to six months. Once you and your boss agree on a promotion plan, remember to get it in writing.

At some point in your early career, it's inevitable that you will be denied advancement. The circumstances vary. Maybe you will ask your manager for a promotion, and she will turn you down outright. Perhaps a higher-level position will open up and one of your colleagues will be slated for it instead of you. It's also possible that your performance review or promotion plan says you are due for advancement, but your boss thinks you still have some work to do before moving ahead. In any case, being denied a promotion can be disappointing and hurtful. However, it does not mean that your boss doesn't like you, or that the company doesn't recognize your contributions. Often, promotion decisions have more to do with the politics of the organization than with you as an individual. It's vital that you don't demonstrate your displeasure, because the "powers that be" might be watching to see how you react. Instead, take an honest look at the reasons behind the decision, and work to overcome real and perceived weaknesses so that you can be successful at the next opportunity.

The "Unofficial" Promotion

> Last year my boss increased the scope of my responsibilities without officially promoting me. My new job required me to interface with clients a lot, so my old title didn't really fit. One customer even said that my business card confused him. I was fed up, so I took the plunge and changed my title in my e-mail signature and on my business cards. My boss eventually got the hint and promoted me.
>
> Henry, 27, Virginia

It happens all the time. You're one of the top performers in your department, but for one reason or another, your boss doesn't promote you. Here are some suggestions for handling some of the more mystifying scenarios:

1. **Your boss keeps giving you new responsibilities, and everyone recognizes that you are operating at a higher level.** Maybe your boss doesn't have the authority to promote you, or maybe she is at the next rung on the ladder so there's nowhere for you to go. It's also possible that your boss doesn't feel a sense of urgency when it comes to your career growth. Talk to your boss frankly about a promotion or compensation appropriate for your new level of responsibility (see "Asking for a Raise," page 186). If that doesn't work, use the visibility tactics described in Chapter 4 to alert the higher-ups to how well you're doing. Really stuck? You may have to roll the political dice and go above your

boss by asking for a meeting with your department head. Just make sure that you frame the conversation in terms of your career development rather than the promotion you want, and that you also keep your boss informed.

2. **You have mastered all of the responsibilities in your job description.** A job well done in the corporate world is not like a great SAT score—it doesn't necessarily predict future success. To get promoted these days, you have to master the skills associated with your current position and, to a great extent, the responsibilities of the next level. In other words, you have to prove that you can add value to a higher-level job before your company will pay you for doing it. If you don't know what's involved in taking your skills and responsibilities up a notch, ask someone in your desired position to act as your mentor and allow you to shadow him for a bit. Don't just observe, though. You'll learn more quickly by actively participating and trying things on your own. As you grow more confident, start acting as though you've already been promoted. If you play your cards right, official recognition will be a natural conclusion.

3. **You are so good at your job that you're the only person who can do it justice.** It's easy for an ambitious twenty-something to get stuck in this trap. If you make yourself irreplaceable, how can the company afford to lose you to a new role? Get out of this one by handpicking a junior member of your team to take your place, either officially or unofficially. Training someone else to do your job as well as you serves two purposes: 1) you'll convince your boss that your job will be left in good hands, and 2) you'll also show her that you're management material.

4. **Over the last few review cycles, you've been promoted like clockwork.** Maybe you've been lucky so far and were appropriately rewarded for stellar performance. Remember that each time you take on a new position, you start from scratch. Just because you were promoted last year and have a great reputation does not mean you have the right combination of skill, visibility, and opportunity to succeed at the next level. Harry Chambers, author of *Getting Promoted: Real Strategies for Advancing Your Career*, reminds us that we are not entitled to anything, and also that dues are never paid in full. Rather, we must campaign for reelection through tangible achievement every day.

Be Careful What You Wish For

If you're reading this book, chances are you are the type of person who can't get promoted soon enough. You probably think you're ready for the next level right now, and you might be frustrated with your management for failing to recognize this fact. The truth is, though, if we twenty-somethings were promoted every time we thought we deserved it, we would all be vice presidents by our 30th birthdays. We all have to learn that the world doesn't work that way, and the sooner we do, the happier we'll be with the way our careers are progressing.

A high school teacher of mine once said, "You don't know what you don't know." In our 20s we don't realize that, smart as we are and quickly as we catch on, we don't have the wisdom or experience to handle the more complicated responsibilities of middle managers in the corporate world. Bosses who make us wait a year or two to get to the next level are usually doing us a favor. When it comes to promotion, you have to be careful what you wish for. I've seen young employees move up and up until they are in way over their heads. The same "lucky" individuals who make us so jealous, often fail outright or self-destruct from the stress of avoiding failure.

At the end of the day you have to ask yourself, "What's the rush?" Of course you want to get to the next level—as well you should. But is your career really going to fall to pieces if it doesn't happen tomorrow? Because you'll probably be in the workforce until you're in your 60s, you have the next 40 years to cope with the anxiety of answering to the big guns, being a slave to your pager, and sitting on top of a team of people who depend on you for their job satisfaction and financial livelihood. Rather than demanding that your career move at the speed of light, why not relax your grip and concentrate on learning everything you can at your current level so that you'll be better prepared for the next? And while you're at it, enjoy having zero decision-making power, relatively normal working hours, and the freedom to go to the bathroom without affecting the company's bottom line. Once you become a corporate superstar, you'll give anything to have these days back.

Handling Setbacks

If you've chosen a career in corporate business, you will inevitably experience some type of setback. You'll be moving along—making great progress, and growing by leaps and bounds every day—and then, suddenly, you'll be dealt a blow. And whether your pet project is canceled, your performance review is a bust, you get turned down for a promotion, or you're asked to leave the company, setbacks hurt big time. You're de-motivated, disillusioned, and pissed as hell. You might not feel like doing anything for a few days except watching MTV, munching on Doritos, and wallowing in self-pity. This response is both normal and appropriate, provided it's short-lived. In his book *Emotional Intelligence at Work*, Hendrie Weisinger tells us that *resiliency*, or the ability to bounce back, is what differentiates people who deal with setbacks effectively from those who don't. Everyone goes through career setbacks, but some people handle them in creative, positive, and rewarding ways, while others sulk, become bitter, and give up on their big-picture goals. As you can imagine, the former individuals are happier overall, and they have more successful careers too.

When you're lying on the ground and your job is stomping all over you, it can be pretty hard to pick yourself up and get moving again. Nevertheless, if you start thinking of yourself as a victim or allow yourself to lapse into prolonged negativity, you won't be hurting anyone except yourself. Worrying until you get sick, abusing alcohol or drugs, or denying that you've reached an impasse won't help either. The best strategy for making a comeback is to recognize the reality of the situation, acknowledge your feelings, and find a way to cope productively. Here are some tips that have gotten me through my darkest career days:

1. **Remind yourself that, in a month, this will be a memory.** When setbacks happen, the tendency is to feel as though your bad luck will last forever. By keeping in mind that the situation is temporary, you'll be strong enough emotionally to take the necessary steps to overcome your misfortune.

2. **Recognize that a setback does not make you a total failure.** Treat your setback as the isolated incident that it is. Regardless of what happened, chances are it's not going to significantly affect your life one way or the other. And I don't know any successful people who've learned the right way to do things without trying several wrong ways first.

3. **Care for your self-esteem.** Your identity and self-worth are too precious to leave in the hands of the volatile corporate world. Your job does not define who you are. You existed before it, and you will exist after it. In the meantime, rather than focusing on your own inadequacies, remind yourself that you are doing the best you can under the current circumstances.

4. **Reach out to your support systems.** During a crisis, it always helps to know you are not alone and that you are justified in feeling the way you do. Instead of withdrawing from the people you care about, make an effort to connect with them and lean on them for support. Your network of friends and family is most critical, but you can receive comfort and insight from spiritual support systems and prayer as well.

5. **Look for humor in the situation.** Having a good laugh can counteract the effects of stress and restore your sense of perspective and your ability to think clearly. It's been proven that when one is happy, the body recovers more quickly from the biological arousal of upsetting emotions. Use whatever humor floats your boat—corny, silly, dry, satirical—as long as it makes you crack a smile.

6. **Be good to your body.** As I've talked about, regular exercise and relaxation techniques (such as stretching, meditating, or yoga) are great ways to reduce negativity and get back on track. Eating reasonable portions of healthy foods can also increase your overall well-being while you are recovering from your setback.

7. **Commit yourself to a new project.** New goals and projects provide fresh perspective and a sorely needed dose of enthusiasm. You'll be motivated to work harder, and will probably be too busy to think much about your setback.

Experiencing a setback doesn't have to be a bad thing. Gail Sheehy, author of *Pathfinders*, who spent years studying what makes happy people tick, offers this gem of optimism: The earlier that we fail at something and our egos crack, the sooner we see that we won't die from it. We realize that our identities will build, show blemishes, suffer injuries, and repair themselves...again and again. Therefore, the best thing that can happen to most people is to fail a little, early in life. As we age and collect more years of experience working in business, the things that seem like mountains now will become smaller and smaller until they barely register as blips on the radar screen. Fortunately, this means our setbacks won't always be so traumatizing.

The Dreaded Reorg

We have a new CEO, and our entire organization is being overturned as we speak. The worst part is that he's talking about moving corporate headquarters to another state! I don't know *what* I'm going to be doing or *where* I'm going to be doing it, and the waiting is killing me. I haven't slept through the night since I found out about this, and I always feel like I'm on the verge of getting sick. I've lived in Colorado all my life, and everything I've ever known is here. I don't know what I'll do if I have to move.

Blair, 26, Colorado

The corporate world wouldn't be the fun place it is without the tribal ritual known as the *reorganization* (aka reorg). A corporate reorg usually follows when new management takes over or existing management decides to change the way the company does business. What does it potentially mean to you? Oh nothing much—except a new job, a new boss, new employees, and maybe even a new place to live. Reorgs don't happen in every company, and they don't always affect everyone in the organization. Depending on management objectives, one division might be restructured while the rest are left untouched. Some companies, however, make reorg an annual event. Regardless of how the current organization is functioning, they insist that change is good and that it can't hurt to stir things up a little. Some also see regular reorgs as an efficient way to shift talent around to best suit the company's needs.

Human beings are not big fans of change, so it shouldn't surprise anyone that the majority of corporate employees don't like reorgs. And life being the way it is, reorgs tend to happen when you're cruising along in your job and everything is going just swell. They'll often strike for no discernable reason, and you'll be left to pick up the pieces of your career. When you're an ambitious twenty-something on the move, an unsolicited change in the landscape you've learned to navigate can be extremely frustrating. You may feel as though all of your recent achievements are for naught. Realize that reorgs aren't personal. Corporate organizations are huge machines, and it's likely your upper management didn't consider how the restructuring would affect you individually.

Reorgs are tough on everyone involved, and how you conduct yourself in the aftermath says a lot about you as an employee. If you think about it, you have two choices: 1) you can leave the company, or 2) you can stay and add value to the new organization. If you choose the latter option, it's critical that you are perceived as flexible, capable, and supportive of the company's direction. When the rug has been pulled out from underneath you and you are thrust into an unfamiliar work situation, it's tempting to develop a bad attitude and express your displeasure to those around you. If there is ever a time to remember your corporate persona, it's now. Reorgs mean new faces, lots of first impressions, and extra scrutiny from senior managers watching to see how the staff is adjusting to the changes. Feel yourself slipping? Use the survival strategies I talked about in Chapter 6 (such as banishing the *shoulds* and taking care of your body) for a boost of positive energy.

If you know a reorg is coming, but you don't have the details, the best thing you can do is anticipate the change and prepare for it as best as you can. Allow yourself to get used to the idea of a new work situation gradually, and begin to think about new opportunities that could arise as a result of the reorg. Consider how you will deal with the worst-case scenario and create a plan of attack for getting through it. Once that's done, recognize that the situation is out of your control and forget about it for the time being. Worrying will not increase the likelihood of a favorable outcome. Instead, you'll most likely drive yourself nuts in the process.

Learning to roll with the punches is especially valuable when it comes to surviving corporate reorgs. Think about it this way: If you were in a sinking ship a few miles from the shore, would you just sit in the hull and complain? Would you wring your hands in despair and jump over the side? No, by golly—you would put on a life jacket and swim your heart out!

Chapter 8 Take Home Points

✓ **Prepare for performance reviews.** Objectives for your performance review should include soliciting feedback on your progress, identifying new goals and growth opportunities, and hammering out a long-term promotion plan. While you can't reasonably expect to be promoted after every review, you should at least leave with an understanding of where your current responsibilities are leading.

✓ **Do your homework before asking for a raise.** When asking your boss for a raise, be prepared with a list of ways you have contributed to the company that have positively impacted the bottom line. Look at the situation from your company's point of view, and then ask yourself if you've performed at such a high level that your company should shell out more assets to keep you.

✓ **Be realistic about your career goals.** Remember that advancing to a higher level means more responsibility and less freedom. Rather than demanding that your career move at the speed of light, relax your grip and concentrate on learning everything you can at your current level so that you'll be better prepared for the next.

✓ **Learn to cope with setbacks.** What differentiates people who deal with setbacks effectively from those who don't is *resiliency*, or the ability to bounce back and cope with life's challenges in creative, positive, and rewarding ways.

Chapter 9

You're the Boss Now!

At some point in your 20s, you will probably receive a promotion that lands you a position where people report directly to *you*. You are now officially someone's boss, and you find yourself having substantial control over his or her destiny. You'll probably be ecstatic, running around your home singing, "At last! At last! I'm not the peon anymore! And I won't make the same mistakes my manager made with me. No way, I know better. I'm going to be the best boss in the world!"

There's only one problem: You don't know better. How could you? In many companies, new managers are initiated with no training whatsoever. This is why there are so many bad ones. Being an effective boss requires a skill set that few people possess naturally, and mastering it is like learning algebra: Watching other people do it isn't enough. In fact, once the excitement from your promotion dies down, you may panic as you realize you have no idea what to do with your new employee. Suddenly your existence in the corporate world has become more complex. Pre-promotion, it was tough enough to successfully steer your own career and keep yourself out of trouble. Now you have to do the same things times two because you are accountable for what your new employee does—and does not—achieve. It's a big responsibility, and one that you must assume carefully if you want to sustain your upward mobility.

This chapter will help you navigate those bewildering first months as a new manager. I'll talk about how to set the stage for a good relationship with your new employee and how you can help her establish goals. I will then go through some of the important aspects of good management—from delegating tasks and communicating effectively, to resolving performance issues and motivating a team. If you have access to a training course to supplement what you read here, I recommend taking advantage of it. Strong leadership skills are not easy to develop or maintain, and you'd be surprised how quickly you can slip back into old habits. When it comes to being the best manager possible, there's no such thing as too many refreshers.

Starting on the Right Foot

When you are assigned a new employee, you should sit down with him for an informal conversation. Taking the employee to lunch is a nice touch, and it will give you the chance to get to know him. Establishing rapport is key, but there is a strategic purpose for this get-together. Remember what I said about first impressions in Chapter 2? Your first meeting with a new employee will demonstrate exactly what kind of boss you will be, and it will influence all interactions from that point on. Use this opportunity to let your employee know right off the bat how you prefer to work and what you expect from him. If the employee is new to the company, you are also responsible for ensuring that he understands his role in the context of the larger organization.

Similarly, you should communicate your boundaries for acceptable conduct and performance as soon as possible. For example, clue him in right away if your company is super strict about arriving to work on time. The first time he slips, subtly let him know that there will be consequences if the behavior continues. Emphasize the importance of meeting project deadlines and observing the organizational hierarchy at the start of your relationship, and no later. I know a lot of managers who desperately want their new employees to like them, so they put up with all kinds of no-no's—from insubordination to mediocre performance—without saying a word. As you can imagine, these managers are always the ones who later complain that their employees don't respect their authority or aren't meeting performance expectations.

Human nature dictates that even hardworking employees may test your boundaries to see what they can get away with. You can save yourself future frustration by guiding your new employee gently but firmly in the right direction. If you're worried about being perceived as the bad guy, remember that employees prefer straightforward, timely feedback to mixed messages, passive-aggressive slighting, or a bad review that comes out of nowhere. Your employee may not always love what you have to say, but he can't fault you for delivering constructive messages in the spirit of goodwill. It wasn't so long ago that you were in his shoes, so simply remember how you wanted to be treated then, and let your instinct be your guide.

A Young Life Is in Your Hands

> My boss is a fantastic role model. She is so posi-
> tive and encouraging that I want to do well. If I
> put extra effort into a project, I know she'll no-
> tice and appreciate it. I'm always a little hesitant
> to try new things because I'm afraid I'll screw
> up, but my boss is great about helping me work
> through the issues so that I don't have to go in
> cold. She's confident in my abilities, which, in
> turn, makes me more confident in myself.
>
> Jori, 23, Vermont

Good management is challenging because every day
you must wear a number of hats. You have to be your
employee's ally, establishing a foundation of trust so that she
is motivated to work hard for you. You must be a director,
staying focused on your department's big-picture objectives
while taking into account your employee's unique contributions. You must also be a coach, supporting your employee's
development through mutual problem-solving. Once you
are assigned an employee, it's not enough to be proactive
about your own workload and direction. You are now also
responsible for mentoring her and helping her forge a rewarding career path.

In Chapter 4, I defined a *goal* as an expectation of
growth and achievement. As I talked about previously,
meaningful career goals are devised by considering
what you want to do, *why* and *when* it should be done,
and *how* success will be measured. BlessingWhite

(*www.blessingwhite.com*), a New Jersey-based consulting firm that has helped 1,500 organizations achieve higher levels of performance and employee commitment, suggests that employee goal-setting is important to effective management because it allows your employee to:

- Understand her responsibilities and what she is expected to achieve.
- Know the criteria on which her performance will be assessed.
- Participate directly in the process, which appeals to her need for collegial support, stimulation, and sharing.

Like your own, your employee's goals should be just challenging enough so that she will continue to put forth effort on an ongoing basis. Early in your relationship, meet with your employee and help her draw up a list of goals. If you are a new manager, it's a good idea to think about this before you're sitting across the desk from your new employee. Taking into account her skill set and any existing goals from previous performance reviews, jot down what you think your employee's goals should be. Stuck? Ask your boss or a senior manager for help.

Write your employee's goals in the format of an informal contract, and add it to her performance review. Note what actions each of you will take to ensure that these goals are achieved. For example, suppose you and your employee agree that she needs to increase her comfort level when speaking in front of large groups. Suggest that she sign up to lead your department's next team meeting and that you help her rehearse her remarks ahead of time. Set timelines and follow-up dates for all goals so that the two of you don't forget about them once you leave the room. In between progress meetings, reinforce your employee's positive steps by rewarding productive behavior immediately and consistently.

Does your employee have a goal you've already achieved? You can help her practice new skills so that she develops the confidence to use them in her work. In his book *Emotional Intelligence at Work*, psychologist Hendrie Weisinger recommends using *modeling*, or demonstrating effective behaviors to be used in a particular situation, and *role-playing*, or simulating through live interaction how a situation might play out. Modeling might sound like a complex psychological term, but it can be as simple as having your employee sit next to you and listen to you call a prospective client. Role-playing in corporate business is less fun than charades, but much more productive. Let's say your employee is nervous about presenting a new idea to a senior member of the department. Acting out the conversation (with you playing the role of senior executive and the employee acting as herself) will help her articulate her thoughts ahead of time and anticipate potential questions and issues.

If you're going to engage in either modeling or role-playing, be sincere and enthusiastic about it. It's your duty to be sensitive to your employee's development—don't ever treat it as a joke. Be cognizant of situations in which your employee may be in over her head, and suggest other alternatives if appropriate. Sometimes you might not have the personal experience needed to assist your employee with her individual goals. If you don't think you can be an effective role model in a particular situation, direct your employee to someone who can. It's always better to admit you don't know something than to lead your employee in the wrong direction.

A key part of your job now is to make sure your employee meets her goals. You may actually be measured on it.

Improve her chances for success by applying all of the people-management tips from Chapter 6. When your employee achieves a goal, don't let the event slip by unnoticed. Praise her, and then encourage her to reach even higher. Basking in the glow of your appreciation and approval, your employee will be motivated to do her best.

Delegating

> This one guy I work with can't delegate a task to save his life. He runs himself ragged while his staff sits around all day doing nothing. I know he does it because he thinks no one can do the job as well as he can, but what happens is that the work doesn't end up getting done at all. Everyone in the department avoids collaborating on projects with his group, which is a shame, because he has some talented people that are totally underutilized.
>
> Terry, 27, Tennessee

You were likely assigned an employee because your workload is too much for one person. Because there are only so many hours in a day, it makes sense to hand off as many assignments as possible. However, many twenty-something managers resist delegating tasks, even if they are in danger of drowning. Some of these reasons are probably close to your heart:

- As the senior team member, you'll do a better job because you know the subject matter and the company's resources inside out.

- It's easier and less time-consuming to do the task yourself than to explain the assignment to your employee.
- You're afraid your employee will screw up the assignment and it will reflect badly on you.
- Your boss likes to micromanage, so you don't want to lose control over the process.
- You like doing a particular task and don't want to give it up.

Any or all of these factors might play a role in your particular situation. That's why delegating work is one of the most challenging managerial skills for a perfectionist twenty-something to develop. Case in point: When I first became a supervisor, I held my cards so close to the vest that my poor employee, Danny, had no idea what was going on. I didn't trust him enough to share the work, so Danny had no choice but to sit in his cube and twiddle his thumbs. After a few months, I developed the reputation of being a bottleneck—assignments arrived in my office and never came out. No one in the department was happy with this situation. I was so stressed that my hair was standing on end, my colleagues were annoyed because they had to go around me to get things done, and Danny felt useless and de-motivated.

I eventually figured out that properly leveraging Danny's contribution did not mean wasting his time with "safe" tasks, such as raiding the mailroom, or giving him ultra-specific instructions on how to do the smallest assignment. Rather, I had to invest time in helping him branch out, so that he could become a self-sufficient member of our team. The day Danny was promoted was one of the best moments of my career, because it was proof that I'd finally mastered the art of delegation. Once I offered

Danny guidance based on what I knew, and then gave him the freedom to approach tasks in his own way, he actually learned something! Here is an example of the process I used to make it happen:

Step 1: *Plan a task to delegate based on your employee's knowledge, skills, and willingness.*

> **Example:** "Danny is really organized and a great multitasker. He did a stellar job helping me with the Widget World booth last month, and I know he's interested in attending a trade show on the West Coast. I think I'll put him in charge of managing our booth at the Widget Symposium. I can see Danny moving into a show management role as early as next year, and I feel that this project would be an excellent jumping off point."

Step 2: *Clearly state the expectations and requirements of the project.*

> **Example** (*to Danny*): "I'd like for you to manage our booth at the Widget Symposium in California in October. As you know from working with me on the Widget World booth last month, we have an approved procedure for coordinating the components and staffing of the booth. However, I would love to see what creative ideas you can come up with for our corporate demo and our visitor giveaways. You'll need to be on-site October 4–8, and I expect planning for the booth to take approximately half of your time in the month leading up to the show."

Step 3: *Explain why the task is important and what you hope your employee will get out of it.*

Example (*to Danny*): "The VP of Corporate Communications considers the Widget Symposium one of the top five annual events for generating company visibility. I hope the project will give you valuable experience working with senior executives and managing vendor relationships. As you move into full-time show management, these skills will be critical."

Step 4: *Empower your employee by asking for his feedback on the best way to accomplish the task.*

Example (*to Danny*): "What do you think about managing this booth by yourself? How do you want to approach reviewing the show's marketing strategy and then getting everyone together for a preliminary planning meeting?"

Step 5: *Suggest a few resources your employee might use to get the job done, but be careful not to micromanage.*

Example (*to Danny*): "You should definitely take another look at the booth planning procedure document we followed for Widget World last month. I will also e-mail you a list of all the internal staff and vendors we worked with on last year's Widget Symposium."

Step 6: *Set target dates for follow-up and completion, and ask your employee to develop an action plan.*

Example (*to Danny*): "I know the details of planning a booth can be overwhelming. To keep the project manageable, why don't you draft an action plan? We can meet on Monday afternoon to go over it."

Step 7: *Meet with your employee regularly to monitor progress, expressing confidence in his ability.*

> **Example** (*to Danny*): "The action plan looks great, Danny. You're doing a terrific job so far and I know the marketing people are impressed with you. Can we meet twice a week until the show, so I can answer any questions you have?"

Step 8: *Evaluate the results and offer constructive feedback.*

> **Example** (*to Danny*): "The booth's execution was flawless and the ChapStick giveaways yielded at least 100 more leads than usual. The VP of Corporate Communications thought you'd been doing this for years! I know all of the last-minute changes were challenging, but your organization and flexibility allowed us to pull it off. Next time, I'd just suggest coordinating an on-site booth staff meeting so you can make sure everyone has their schedules in advance."

● ● ●

If you want your employee to be receptive to future assignments and enjoy working on your team, be appreciative of his efforts and allow him to manage projects independently. Your role is to offer direction and a supportive ear—*not* to get involved in all of the nitty-gritty aspects of the task. The first few times you try to delegate an important assignment will probably be difficult. Just keep in mind the end goal. The more autonomy and decision-making authority your employee has, the faster he'll acquire expertise that will make your job easier!

Countering Objections

Tasks that you assign to your employee may not always be received with open arms. However, you can't back down just because your employee objects to an assignment. She will learn that expressing displeasure will get her out of any responsibility she doesn't like, and, next thing you know, she'll be walking all over you. A successful leader is well-liked and still manages to get things done. You can become one by mastering how to handle objections. Suppose you are a sales manager for a pharmaceutical company. Your employee, a sales representative, does not want to attend an out-of-town bioscience training seminar because she is too busy. You need her to complete the course so that she has the knowledge base to take on two important accounts. Let's illustrate how you might handle this situation using a technique advocated by leadership consulting firm BlessingWhite:

Step 1: *Press for specifics to get to the heart of the concern.*

> **You:** "You mentioned that you don't want to take the seminar because you have too much on your plate. What deadlines do you have next week? If you brief me ahead of time, I'm sure that I or someone else can cover your 'to do's.' You wouldn't have to worry about your other work at all. Is there another reason you don't want to go?"

> **Employee:** "Well, actually, the seminar just comes at a really bad time. My boyfriend just got out of the hospital. He had an appendectomy. He's fine now, but I'm worried that if I leave town, something will happen."

Step 2: *Show that you understand by paraphrasing or empathizing in a warm and genuine tone.*

> **You:** "The last thing you want to do is leave someone you love when he's sick. You must be afraid that if you go to the seminar, you won't be able to check on him as often and that you'll be too far away to help if there are any complications."

> **Employee:** "Exactly. I mean, it's not like he's alone. His mother lives a few blocks away and calls every day. It just makes me anxious, you know?"

Step 3: *Respond with the appropriate facts and/or benefits about the task.*

> **You:** "Sure. Well, listen, I'd really like for you to attend this seminar. Your career here is skyrocketing. I know you really want to take on some of the higher-profile bioscience accounts. I think that you're ready, but this training is required before you can start. Unfortunately, the seminar won't be given for another six months. I would hate to hold up your progress that long."

> **Employee:** "I really do want to move up, and those accounts will help me do it sooner rather than later. I guess I didn't realize why you were pushing me to fly out for this training. To be honest, I didn't see it as a priority. I'm going to explain the situation to my boyfriend's mother. Maybe she'll be willing to look in on him a little more often than usual."

Step 4: *Test for acceptance.*

> **You:** "So is it okay if I go ahead and sign you up for the seminar? My admin can book your travel so that you're back on Friday in plenty of time to spend the weekend with your boyfriend."

> **Employee:** "I think we can do that. Thanks."

•••

Recall the Win/Win approach from Chapter 7. Your employee will be much more likely to cooperate with you if you make her *want* to do what you're proposing. Now, let's be real here—there won't be a Win for your employee in every task you ask her to complete. Sometimes, you will have to delegate an assignment that is just plain undesirable. When you're the bearer of bad news and you know it, it's best to get right to the point. Explain the situation and what needs to be done as positively as you can. Acknowledge your employee's feelings about what you're communicating, and encourage her to participate in finding an acceptable solution. Even if you're as frustrated as she is, don't show it. One of the hallmarks of a true leader is to make the best of unfortunate scenarios without breaking a sweat.

Criticism: It's a Dirty Job...

For me, the most difficult part of being a manager is delivering criticism. Even if it's given nicely, it's still criticism, and I know that *I* don't like receiving it from *my* boss. I've realized, though, that if I never suggest how my employee can improve, he won't. He'll assume that my constant positive reinforcement means he's doing everything perfectly, and he won't bother to learn the new skills required to progress. And then what kind of manager would I be?

Criticism is necessary to any manager/employee relationship, but you should never bang him over the head with it. You are not a playground bully, so always make sure to phrase your comments constructively. Begin with a positive statement about your employee's performance, and do not follow it with the word *but*. The *but* erases the good intentions behind your original comment and diminishes the credibility of the criticism to come. *But* may seem harmless, yet it has the power to anger people like nothing else. Prevent your employee's negative reaction by changing the word *but* to the word *and*. For instance:

Example #1:

"Dave, your Website design is very sophisticated, *but* I'd like to see you replace the pastels with dark colors to enhance the effect."

Example #2:

"Dave, your Website design is very sophisticated, *and* I'd like to see you replace the pastels with dark colors to enhance the effect."

See how much nicer Example #2 sounds?

Of course, some people are super sensitive and have trouble swallowing direct criticism of any kind. My colleague recently shared a wonderful tactic that has worked for me on several occasions. If you want to improve a person in a certain respect, act as though he's already behaving the way you want him to. He will want to prove that you were right to think so highly of him. For example, suppose you want your employee to take better notes at team meetings. Take him aside and tell him that you wish you were as organized as he is. "I don't know how you keep track of everything that goes on in those meetings," you could add. "Your notes saved my life last week when the General Manager asked for the statistics that the Investor Relations Group presented." Your employee will think about your compliment every time he goes to a team meeting—and you can bet that the quality of his notes will be better for it. After all, you told him that you love his notes, and he won't want to disappoint the boss.

Addressing Performance Issues

A *performance problem* may be defined as a situation in which your employee's work does not meet your expectations. Maybe she turns in her weekly reports with typos, freezes up when it's her turn to present in team meetings, or lets important deadlines slide. Telling employees to shape up is such a sticky wicket that many managers steer away from it entirely. The reasons vary. Some managers genuinely like the employee with the performance problem, and they don't want to offend her. Others are simply unable to tackle uncomfortable situations head-on.

Whatever the motivation, a huge percentage of managers keep their gripes to themselves. They go about their business, allowing their disapproval to simmer while their employees continue to be ineffective. Remember that people are not mind readers. If you don't tell your employee what she's doing wrong, she won't fix it. And if she doesn't fix it, either you or your department could suffer a breakdown. Waiting until her review to discuss the performance problem is not a good idea either. By the time the assessment period rolls around, you will have had to cope with the problem for who knows how many months. A review-based conversation also means that your employee won't have the chance to correct the problem before it is noted in her permanent record and affects her compensation.

You should address performance problems in a timely fashion, but you don't want to jump down your employee's throat every time she makes a mistake either. How can you strike a good balance? The first time your employee commits an infraction (provided it's not something to fire her over), let it go. Wait and see if the incident was just a fluke or if your employee corrects it on her own. However, if the issue rears its ugly head on an ongoing basis, it may be time to sit down with her and address it. The following steps will guide you through the process:

Step 1: *Begin with a positive comment—and mean it.*

> **Example:** "The General Manager was really impressed with your presentation this morning. He thought you were very articulate and natural in front of the podium."

Step 2: *Explain the performance problem by citing specific instances.*

> **Example:** "You're an excellent impromptu speaker, and I'd like to see you prepare for your presentations in advance so that you can use concrete examples and statistics to back up your arguments. This morning, for example, you needed to back up your claims about growth in manufacturing with market research and third-party support. And a few weeks ago, you briefed our lobbyist partners on our product strategy without citing any specifics about our play in the government space."

Step 3: *Tactfully point out potential consequences if the problem continues.*

> **Example:** "I'm concerned that if you continue to do these types of presentations on the fly, a client will call you on it and we could have an embarrassing situation on our hands. As poised as you are, I can't put you in front of

customers if it could compromise the company's reputation."

Step 4: *Ask for your employee's feedback in solving the problem.*

Example: "What do you think is the best way to plan for your next presentation?"

Step 5: *Offer any suggestions you have for solving the problem.*

Example: "Can I suggest that you brainstorm an outline for each presentation a week before you're scheduled to deliver it? I think this approach will help you fill in the holes and anticipate questions ahead of time. You'll also have time to consult with the Market Research Group so that they can provide you with the supporting data you need."

Step 6: *Work with your employee to develop an action plan.*

Example: "If you can complete the outline for the upcoming business presentation by next Tuesday, we can meet to go over it. I'll give you an extension on your other deadlines so that you have time to thoroughly research your main arguments. Once you've prepared your PowerPoint slide show, we can rehearse the entire presentation in the conference room, and I can help you with any parts that still need some tweaking. Sound like a plan?"

Step 7: *Support your employee's efforts to change.*

Example: "Thanks so much for working with me here. Good public speakers are rare, and I know that you're going to become one of our best."

Step 8: *Follow up and reward improvements.*

Example: "We won the new account largely due to your efforts. Your presentation was rock solid, and I know the clients were impressed with your in-depth knowledge of their business. How would you like to work directly with the General Manager on our annual briefing for the CEO?"

• • •

When it comes to addressing performance issues, the key word is *performance*. No matter what your employee's problem is, you must look at it in the context of her overall contribution. For example, suppose she does outstanding work and always hands in her assignments early, but she consistently breezes in at 9:30 a.m. Before you engage her in a dialogue about her tardiness, consider if it's worth it. If her lateness is not affecting the quality of her work and your boss won't notice because he works out of another office, you might be wise to avoid a confrontation. You know the old saying: If it ain't broke, don't fix it!

Encouraging Open Communication

I really couldn't tell you what my boss expects, because I never hear from him. He works out of another office, and when he does come here, he spends all of his time in meetings. We only talk so that he can review me twice a year, and so that he can tell me about the raise I'm not getting. Fortunately, I know what my role is, and I am able to do my own thing with a minor amount of direction. I think I do decent work. I just wish that my boss was more accessible, so that I could know for sure.

Anthony, 25, California

In Chapter 5, I talked extensively about techniques for good communication. I discussed the importance of *assertiveness*, or the ability to stand up for your rights, opinions, ideas, and desires while respecting those of others. I also covered specific strategies for leveraging three communication vehicles—writing, speaking, and listening—to sustain positive work relationships. It's in your best interest to communicate well with everyone you work with, but it's most critical when it comes to interacting with a direct employee. As the manager, the onus is on you to make sure information is shared, and if you fall down on the job, your employee's performance and morale may suffer.

Earlier in this chapter, I suggested how to set a precedent for good communication. Keeping the lines open over time, however, is more challenging than you think. When you're a busy manager, the tendency is to stop talking to your employee. You're tied up with your own assignments, and you expect your employee to be off and running with his. After you provide initial direction on a task, you assume that he knows what he's doing. You don't check in with him, and you don't ask him to check in with you.

As time goes by and your employee doesn't see you for a while, he begins to perceive you as unapproachable. He is working in a vacuum, and it's anyone's guess whether or not his performance is actually on target. In the absence of feedback from his manager, he might feel confused or de-motivated. Pretty soon, he might stop making meaningful contributions to the team, and his career growth will slam to a screeching halt.

Don't get me wrong: Communication breakdowns are not always the manager's fault. Some employees are notoriously closemouthed and will refrain from volunteering any information about their work. Others will give you data that you don't need. For the sake of group performance, you must solicit timely and relevant feedback from your employee. Set up weekly or biweekly meetings with him to discuss the status of his projects and to provide guidance on issues he may be facing. Leadership consulting firm BlessingWhite recommends asking targeted questions during these meetings to draw your employee out, and to encourage informative responses:

Factual Questions: These questions should be asked when you are looking for specific data or statistics. Because these questions are straightforward, have a reason for asking them and don't make your inquiry sound like an interrogation. Factual questions can be *open* or *closed*.

Value Questions: These questions should be asked to find out how your employee thinks or feels about a particular issue. They help you understand your employee's point of view and determine areas that might need further exploration. Value questions can be *open* or *closed*.

Open Questions: These questions begin with a *what*, *when*, *where*, *why*, and *how*. They cannot be answered with a *yes* or a *no*. These questions allow for the greatest range of responses and provide the greatest opportunity for your employee to express his ideas freely.

Closed Questions: These questions can be answered with a *yes* or a *no*. They allow you to ask for more specific information and narrow the range of responses, which can help keep the discussion on track and moving forward.

●●●

Finally, let your employee know that you are always there for him. If he comes by your office and you don't have time to chat, try to set aside time that day, if possible.

Remember that the younger your employees are, the more sensitive they tend to be, so be gentle with your criticism. Take advantage of every opportunity to mentor your employee, and allow him to benefit from your experience. Touch base with him often—always graciously—and he will feel comfortable coming to you. I think you'll find that when you are proactive about establishing a pattern of open communication, information exchange is easy, and your team is happier and more productive.

Managing Teams

As an employee, I suffered from a certain curse: My strong work ethic compelled me to do the best job possible on *every* assignment—even if it was the worst assignment possible. However, some of the people in my group were particularly lazy when it came to the work no one wanted to do. After my boss got burned a few times, she started giving all the unpleasant tasks to me because she knew I would get them done. I was actually being punished for my performance, and it felt horrible. Now as a manager, I remember that this is no way to treat people I want to keep around. All of the work is doled out equally, but the more appealing tasks are used to reward hardworking employees. My strongest people feel appreciated—and the others are motivated to do better so that they, too, can get the favorable assignments.

Susan, 28, Texas

J. Richard Hackman, author of *Leading Teams*, defines a *team* as a set of people who view themselves as team members and share accountability toward some outcome. As a team manager, you are responsible for ensuring that your employees understand the purpose of the group and how to leverage their own expertise to achieve the group's objectives. Previously, I talked about supervising teams in the context of project management. Your mission is raised a level when you are chosen to manage a team permanently, and when your employees rely on you for total job direction rather than individual project direction. Hackman offers the following recommendations for negotiating the team terrain:

- Maintain a stable group. (People need to be on the team long enough to know how to work well together.)
- Communicate a clear direction, while giving the team freedom to figure out how best to accomplish the group's objectives.
- Support your team by sharing information often, making training readily available, and by providing consistent rewards.
- Prevent organizational roadblocks by collaborating with senior executives to make sure that the right conditions in place.

In my experience, leaders must keep in mind a few additional guidelines to effectively manage a team. First, you must treat team members equally. This might sound like a no-brainer, but you'd be surprised how easy it is to play favorites or choose to spend more time with certain individuals. After all, some of your employees will have working styles or personalities similar to yours, so you'll find it easier to coach and delegate projects to them. However, because your employees will talk to each other, make a concerted effort to share workload, information, and kudos across the board. Also, don't take advantage of the can-do people in your group by giving them twice as much work as everyone else. If some employees aren't pulling their weight, address the issue with each person individually rather than relying on the others to carry them along. And if you're going to reward a certain team member with a raise, a comp day, or a special privilege, do it discreetly so that you don't arouse resentment within the group.

Remember that your employees are not your friends. While it's great to develop a strong rapport with them and to get to know them as individuals, you should be careful about how much information you share about your personal life and how often you get together with them socially outside the office. Your relationships with your employees should always maintain a degree of professionalism. The more the lines blur, the tougher it is to do your job as a manager. For instance, you may find yourself skirting an employee's performance problem because you don't want to jeopardize your friendship with her, or you may tell her something in confidence that she could later claim as inappropriate boss-to-employee communication. Because it's challenging to meet people in your 20s, the office is a natural place to scope out new friendships. You'd be wise, however, to look outside your reporting structure for a new buddy.

Overseeing productive team meetings is another responsibility that separates the strong supervisors from the weak. Two of the biggest gripes I've heard about managers are that they either refuse to have team meetings, or that they run them inefficiently. Recognize that team meetings serve a variety of purposes, including communicating new goals and information, building teamwork, motivating employees, and providing a forum to resolve issues. If you never call your group together as a team, your employees might feel isolated and uninformed, and problem issues may fester because there is no opportunity to clear the air. However, you don't want to have meetings just for the sake of having meetings either. Here are some do's and don'ts for managing effective meetings:

✓ *DO* allow your employees to have a say in determining the agenda for the meeting.

✓ *DO* distribute the agenda ahead of time, making sure to list the specific issues to be discussed.

✓ *DO* plan something special every now and then, such as bringing in lunch or donuts.

✓ *DO* have team members contribute to the meeting by having them provide a status update for their projects.

✓ *DO* keep the tone of the discussion open and positive.

✓ *DO* encourage team members to freely voice their concerns, to listen, and to help one another.

✓ *DO* maintain a big-picture perspective and calmly guide the group toward a consensus or solution if a problem arises.

✓ *DO* consider your team's time pressures and keep the meeting to an hour.

✗ *DON'T* have meetings too often (once a week should be the maximum).

✗ *DON'T* allow team members to interrupt each other or monopolize the discussion with their own opinions.

✗ *DON'T* allow the discussion to wander off topic for too long.

One last piece of advice: If you're in your 20s and are already managing a team, chances are you're on the fast track. You are obviously good at what you do and have earned a pat on the back—but beware the ego. Nobody likes an arrogant manager, and I guarantee that you will be difficult to work with if you insist that you're always right. The people underneath you can teach you something if you're willing to pay attention. Remember this saying from Ralph Waldo Emerson and stay humble: "Every man I meet is my superior in some way. In that, I learn from him."

Chapter 9 Take Home Points

✓ **Make expectations clear up front.** Your first interactions with new employees demonstrate exactly what kind of boss you will be. Use the opportunity to let them know right off the bat how you prefer to work and what you expect from them.

✓ **Teach employees to be self-sufficient.** Invest time teaching your employees what they need to know to become fully functioning members of your team. Show that you appreciate their efforts, and allow then to manage projects independently. Your role is to offer direction and a supportive ear—*not* to micromanage.

✓ **Learn to criticize constructively.** Criticism is necessary to any manager/employee relationship, but you should never bang your employee over the head with it. Phrase your comments constructively. Follow a positive statement about your employee's performance with the word *and* instead of the word *but*. The *but* erases the good intentions behind your original comment and diminishes the credibility of the criticism to come.

✓ **Be meeting savvy.** Set up regular meetings with each of your employees to solicit timely and relevant feedback. Ask targeted questions to prompt discussion about project status, and make sure to provide guidance on issues they may be facing.

Chapter 10

Exit
Stage Left

The U.S. Bureau of Labor Statistics predicts that today's 22-year-old college graduate will have more than eight different employers before she reaches age 32. This means that, on the average, twenty-somethings are changing jobs every 15 months. No doubt about it, this is not your parents' corporate world. Most people their age spent decades working their way up the ladder in the same company—a career path that is virtually unheard of today. The job-jumping craze of the late 1990s may be over, but the job market will continue to be fluid as company loyalty decreases and a forthcoming labor shortage opens more opportunities for ambitious young workers.

Once you've been in your first position a year or two, it may be time to think about making a strategic career move. Why? No matter how well you're perceived in your current role, you'll move up more quickly if you change jobs. Now that you have some experience under your belt, you can command a higher salary, a better title, and more responsibility if you go elsewhere. Your 20s are the best time to make such a move, because you are relatively unencumbered. Most twenty-somethings don't have to worry about how a job switch will affect their children's school schedule or healthcare benefits. You uncover a new opportunity—and carpe diem!

Unfortunately, the decision to leave a job is not always one you have the luxury to make. Sometimes, for reasons you might not be able to control, you may be fired or laid off. In this chapter, I'll discuss how to detect and repair when your job may be on the line. Next, if you're ready for that strategic career move, I'll walk you through some techniques for scoping out a new position inside and outside your current company. I'll also cover good reasons to leave a job that aren't so strategic, such as being in an abusive situation. Finally, I'll talk about ways to make a graceful exit and preserve ties with your employer that will serve you well in the future.

Beware the Pink Slip

I had a feeling my job was in trouble when things started happening in my area that I didn't know about. All of a sudden, other people in my department were calling my clients without keeping me in the loop. This, combined with the fact that I had a new boss, clued me in that something bad was about to go down. I had been a loyal employee for three years and didn't want to leave, so I confronted my boss about it. I told him how committed I was to the new administration and asked him how I could adjust my performance to meet his needs. I think he was a little surprised that I was savvy enough to figure out what was going on. I bent over backwards to please him for a while, and he gave me a break and let me keep my job.

Orrin, 28, Washington

When my friend David was fired two years ago, he saw it coming. He had a new boss whom he clashed with terribly. David had been an excellent employee, but after his new manager started criticizing him all the time, David lost his motivation. Eventually, he was just going through the motions. Once David's manager officially documented his poor performance, David knew his days were numbered. He was not surprised when he received a pink slip a month later.

Some bored or miserable employees might not have the emotional energy to consider whether they might be fired. Maybe it's all they can do to drag themselves to work in the morning. They think about quitting, but because they don't have anywhere else to go, they stick around and put in the minimum effort. Does this describe you? Let this serve as a wake-up call: If you hate it enough and don't do anything to fix the problem, your job is probably in jeopardy. Why? Long-term job dissatisfaction is difficult to hide. Your boss probably knows you're unhappy, and, if the situation continues, she'll probably find a way to get rid of you. Here are some other scenarios that should set off your smoke alarm:

- You received a bad review or were put on probation.
- You are no longer being consulted on new projects.

- Your colleagues are inexplicably ignoring you.
- You have a new boss you don't get along with.
- Your boss has started giving your responsibilities to other people.
- Your colleagues stop including you in relevant meetings.
- You haven't kept your skills current or up to par.
- You haven't accomplished what you were hired to do.
- You don't adapt well to changes within the company.
- You've been told you need an attitude adjustment.
- You don't fit the corporate mold.
- You have a history of acting inappropriately in the office (for example, insubordination or gossiping).
- You committed an unpardonable infraction (for example, cursing out a client or demonstrating overt racism or sexism).

We all go through periods of trouble on the job. Even if one or more of these warning signals applies to you, the black cloud may pass, or you may be able to work through it. Understanding when you're in danger of being fired can only empower you. Whether your job is being threatened by colleagues' perception of wrongdoing or actual wrong-doing, knowing what you're up against will help you determine a course of action. Appropriate resolutions vary. For example, if you've been chastised for bad behavior, you should cease the action immediately and show genuine remorse for any trouble you've caused. Alternatively, if your boss feels you're not producing, you should document your tangible contributions and present them to her at every opportunity. Did your manager give you a performance plan? That piece of paper (or two) should be your new Bible. Live by it. Make sure you measurably improve in each designated area by the deadline noted in the plan.

In most cases, your boss won't fire you without a legitimate reason. Don't give her one. Once you discover where things are not working, swallow your pride and take the necessary steps to protect your career and your future.

Layoff Survival

In the corporate world today, layoffs are so common, it's scary. Companies have to answer to Wall Street and their shareholders, and when an organization fails to meet its projections, a logical first step is to "trim the fat"—or eliminate jobs. Regardless of your reputation or skill set, your company might decide that your position is expendable, and they will send you packing. Usually you will have a lot of people in the same boat as you are because companies typically lay off many employees at the same time. On the one hand, being laid off is easier to stomach than being fired—it's less personal and you often can't do anything to change the decision one way or the other. However, layoffs are more disconcerting because it's harder to see the writing on the wall. Concerned? Keep on the lookout for the following danger signs:

- Top management changes result in a new corporate direction.
- The *Yahoo!* Message Boards are rumbling about layoffs.
- Your company's financial woes are all over the news.

- Your company or department is underperforming.
- Senior executives are spending a lot of time holed up in a conference room.
- Your company has stopped investing in employees' careers via internal training or tuition reimbursement.
- Your department's budget has been drastically cut or eliminated.
- A recent reorg has left you without many of your former responsibilities.

Pay attention to these indicators. You must not permit yourself the luxury of denial or thinking a layoff could never happen to you. If you suspect that you are about to become a victim, take action before you are officially unemployed. Use the tactics from Chapter 1 (such as compiling a power resume and networking for job leads) to get a jump on the situation. In your 20s, you're typically not at a level that warrants a cushy severance package, so create an emergency financial plan that will carry you through a temporary loss of income. While you're at it, investigate post-employment health insurance options such as COBRA, and your company's policy for rolling over 401(k) funds.

Sometimes, a layoff will take you completely by surprise. This is a traumatic experience, but do not allow it to destroy your confidence. Prospective employers recognize that companies are downsizing all over the place, and they will probably not hold a layoff against you. You should have no trouble landing on your feet, provided you start looking for another job right away. Interviewers will appreciate your resilience, whereas they may become skeptical if you stay off the market for too long. So if you're ever laid off, hold your head up high. Look at it as a good opportunity to find a company that truly values your talent and expertise.

Smart Career Moves

> In this economy, I was afraid to quit my job, even though I was beginning to hate life. I basically liked the company I worked for, so I started talking to people about opportunities in other departments. Turns out that one of the managers doing business development had noticed me during the few times we'd worked together. He was building up his team, and he'd heard that I had a good reputation. I didn't tell my current boss about it until the terms of my transfer—which included a promotion and a substantial raise—were nearly finalized. By that time, it was too late for her to try and stop me.
>
> Seth, 24, Delaware

As I've talked about before, few corporate employees today are *lifers*, or individuals who stay at the same company for the duration of their careers. In particular, junior employees are both encouraged and expected to move around during their 20s. Even if you're happy with your job, it always pays to be on the lookout for the next big thing. This way, instead of waiting patiently to be promoted year after year, you can sell your skills to a new employer for a higher title and salary right now. In this section, I'll discuss the mechanics behind smart career moves, including how to transfer to a lateral position within your current organization, and how to scope out opportunities in a new company while you're still employed at the old.

One important caveat before I begin: Be wary of changing jobs *too* often. As a twenty-something in corporate business, you should hold each job for at least a year before you consider a change. Individuals who switch more often become known as chronic job jumpers, and employers avoid these candidates like the plague. When a hiring manager sees a resume listing four jobs in three years, he won't wait to hear your explanation. He'll think that you can't hold down a job, and he will move on to the next person.

If you are a chronic job jumper and find yourself looking for a way out once again, you might want to do some soul-searching. A pattern of unsatisfying work experiences could mean that the problem lies not with the jobs or the companies, but with *you*. Here's an example: In my early career I worked with a woman named Joselyn who was a few years older than me. Joselyn tried in vain to find job satisfaction in a few different positions. Eventually she realized that while her five work situations had been very different, her negative attitude was the one constant. She wasted a lot of time looking high and low for a better job when she should have been focusing on how she could be happier and more effective where she was. Don't let this happen to you.

As you're preparing to make a move, ask yourself the following questions, to ensure that you're leaving for the right reasons. Consider the answers carefully and be realistic!

- Why do you want to look for a new job?
- Are you satisfied doing what you're doing?

- Are you adequately challenged? If not, do you even want to be challenged?
- Do you like the people and work environment?
- Are you fairly compensated?
- Are you treated with respect?
- Are you empowered to do your job effectively?

Transferring Inside the Company

The longer you work at a company, the more exposure you have to different functional areas. As you get to know more players and talk to them about what they do, you may find your interest peaked. There is usually no shortage of opportunities for ambitious and well-regarded twenty-somethings who want to transfer internally. Managers are always looking for good employees with a basic skill set who won't come with huge salary requirements. Also, companies generally prefer to fill open positions by hiring from within. Some even have policies dictating that they must consider qualified internal candidates before they can expand a job search outside the company.

One type of internal transfer is the *lateral move*. In a lateral move, a strong employee takes on a new position at the same level as his former position. Most companies encourage these because they are mechanisms for keeping good people happy and sufficiently challenged without promoting them. Lateral moves also save businesses the cost and risk of bringing in new employees who are unknown commodities. You may want to consider a lateral move if any of the following circumstances apply:

- You're more interested in stretching your wings and experiencing new things than moving up the ladder as fast as possible.

- You feel you are at a dead-end in your current position, and you want to open a new door.
- The company is decreasing its focus on your area, and you want to better position yourself for long-term career growth.
- You're at odds with your manager or a coworker, and you have been unable to resolve the situation.
- You've discovered an opportunity to work in an area that will bring you closer to your big-picture career goals.
- You're being recruited by a manager you would love to work for.

Think a lateral move is right for you? You should certainly go for it. Just keep in mind that, in order to learn about internal opportunities, you will have to do the legwork. You may get lucky and have a savvy manager approach you with a job offer, but, in most cases, you'll be on your own. Start by finding out if your company has a Website or a newsletter that publicizes job openings to employees. Review this outlet religiously. If you see a position that intrigues you, discreetly follow up with the hiring manager. While this process is in motion, keep the prospects coming in by networking with as many senior managers as you can. Get to know them on a personal level, and ask them casually what they're doing in their groups. During these discussions, never criticize your current manager, department, or position. If a manager thinks you're a spoiled brat who's running away from a difficult work situation, he won't want to bring you on board. Phrase your inquiries positively and innocently—you just want to learn, remember?

Scouting out an appropriate opportunity to transfer internally is one thing, but actually making the transition happen is quite another. Here are a couple of tips that will help you. First, just because your company is behind your decision 100 percent doesn't mean your boss will be. Whether you're pursuing a move through human resources or directly with another manager, keep the discussions under wraps until the transfer is close to being finalized. If your boss doesn't want to lose you and finds out what you're up to too early, she may subtly—or not so subtly— block your progress. Once it's time to ink the deal, make sure HR is in the loop so that everyone involved adheres to the agreed-upon transition plan. Don't depend on your old boss and your new boss to work it out amongst themselves. Your old boss may try to hold on to you as long as she can, and, next thing you know, you'll have a major territory war on your hands.

Also, avoid talking about the move to your colleagues before it's official, because you might compromise your reputation in the group if the job falls through. You'll also feel like an idiot. Look at it this way: If your team were going to the Super Bowl, you wouldn't talk about the victory parade until after the game, right? Same goes for your potential hot new job down the hall!

Looking Elsewhere

It's easiest to look for a new job while you're still employed. Makes sense, right? You're more attractive to hiring managers because you're free of the unemployment stigma. And because you're still receiving a steady paycheck, you come across as more discerning. Prospective employers know you're not desperate enough to take a job that's not a good fit.

Before you start talking to anyone about a new job, crystallize your big-picture goals so that you know exactly what you're looking for. Update your resume with all of your new skills and accomplishments. Next, explore the job-search outlets described in Chapter 1 (such as Websites, networking, and headhunters) to get the ball rolling.

Ideally, you will want to do all of your job-searching research outside of business hours, but this just isn't practical. Do what you need to do while on the clock—just be careful that you don't get caught! Surf career Websites discreetly. Don't blindly send your resume all over the Internet or respond to job postings without knowing where they're coming from. And if you can, register with career sites that allow you to protect your listing from your existing employer.

As far as your colleagues are concerned, it should be business as usual. Don't arouse suspicion by changing your patterns. Use sick days to go on interviews if you must, but try to stack up your appointments over a two- or three-day period so you can chalk your absence up to an actual illness. Similarly, if your company dresses in business casual, wearing a suit to work will send a clear signal that you're interviewing during your lunch hour. Change en route instead.

When making calls to potential employers, use a private office or conference room. Set up a separate e-mail account for your job search, and if you need to fax your resume, hit your local Kinkos. Remember that you are still receiving a paycheck from your current company. Don't spend too much time job searching when you should be working, and make sure you're producing on a regular basis. If anything, you should work harder than ever so that you can count on strong references down the road.

While we're on the subject of references, don't ask anyone from your current job to be one. Hopefully you have other options, because it's never a good idea to let people at your company know you're looking. Unless you want your whole office to know about your plans, don't tell a soul—even your closest colleague or your mentor.

As you interact with hiring managers and headhunters, be assertive about what you're looking for. Prospective employers prefer candidates who are in good standing with their current employers, so act like you're happy at your job even if you're not. Your reason for leaving should always be a positive one. For example: You're looking for an opportunity to expand your skill set and take on new challenges.

If you get an offer, think through the logistics before agreeing on a start date. You still have a job and need to give two weeks notice before departing for greener pastures. When you accept a new job, let your current boss know first, as a courtesy, and assure him that you will do everything you can to transition your responsibilities smoothly.

When to Quit Now and Worry Later

After law school, I took an associate position at a city firm. I'd been there about a month when I realized that the place was a total boy's club. All of the guys were 6 feet tall and blond, and the few women there fell all over themselves trying to get in good with the men. The senior lawyers had apparently never heard of an ambitious woman, and they were pretty vocal about putting me in my place. It was disgusting. I guess, technically, I could sue them, but it's not worth the time and effort. I'll just go somewhere that appreciates an associate who's willing to work her butt off.

Darcy, 26, Ohio

In a perfect world you would love your job to death and would only consider leaving for "good" reasons, such as the career opportunity of a lifetime or your spouse's relocation. But at some point in your early career, it's likely that a job won't work out the way you planned. For reasons beyond your control, you may find yourself in a bad work situation that mandates quitting sooner rather than later.

No matter what the trouble is, it's usually best to stick it out until you get something better and are able to jump right into another position. However, as I've talked about, finding new employment takes time. If your work is seriously compromising your mental or physical health and it's torture to go into the office every day, you might not want to wait. After all, no job is worth sacrificing your well-being. Here are some scenarios that may warrant leaving now and worrying about the consequences later:

1. **You are being emotionally abused.** Is an individual at work unnecessarily unfair or cruel to you? Does she ridicule you in front of your colleagues? Does she regularly call you into her office to insult you or ream you out? Don't be fooled: Emotional abuse can be just as damaging as physical abuse. If you feel your self-esteem taking a beating, get out of the situation.

2. **You are being sexually harassed.** Has someone in your company repeatedly approached you in a way that makes you feel uncomfortable? Does he communicate in person or in e-mail in an inappropriate fashion? Has he subtly or overtly promised you advancement or perks in return for sexual favors? You should not grin and bear it, no matter how much of a big shot your offender is.

3. **You have been asked to compromise your integrity.** Is your boss or another authority figure asking you to lie, cheat, or steal? Do your assigned job responsibilities compromise your personal ethics? Don't allow yourself to be pressured into a situation that could ruin your career.

4. **You don't feel safe coming to work.** Is your company located in a dangerous area? Are you afraid to walk to and from the office alone? Are the working conditions harmful or unsanitary? I don't care how much you're getting paid: Your job should not jeopardize your health or security.

Under some circumstances, it might be wise to pay human resources a visit before handing in your resignation. Sometimes, particularly in harassment cases, HR may be able to step in and quietly resolve the issue without costing you your job. In general, though, be wary of complaining to HR. Your HR rep's job is to side with the company you both work for, so don't blindly divulge information to her as though she's your therapist. Even if your situation is objectively horrible, be positive about seeking a resolution, and don't tell your HR rep anything that could be used against you.

Also, remember that when it comes to HR, you can't necessarily count on confidentiality. To be safe, you should assume that anything you say in an HR rep's office will get back to the person or people you're talking about. And if your conflict is with a senior manager, you may not get a fair hearing. When it's "his word against hers," many HR reps will side with the more senior person involved, prejudicing them against you—the junior employee. Now don't get me wrong: Certain issues, such as sexual harassment, need to be confronted, and HR can be a useful ally in helping you do just that. Just keep in mind that the decision to involve HR should not be made lightly, and make sure to think through the consequences before making that call.

Know Your Rights

Life in the corporate world isn't always fair, but it's helpful to know when your workplace has crossed a legal line and when the company is well within its rights. For example, did you know that in most states in America, employers have the right to discriminate against employees because they are too young? Yes, it's true. The U.S. federal law only protects people from discrimination if they are over 40 and considered too old.

Have you ever heard the legal definition of *insubordination*? The word *insubordinate* can be dissected as *in* = not, and *subordinate* = subject to the authority of another. Someone who is legally insubordinate refuses to recognize the authority of the employer, which can mean anything from cursing your boss out to refusing to complete a task that you consider unimportant.

And get a load of this one: In North America, most employees are *at-will*. This means that representatives of a company hire you because they feel like it, and when your employment no longer suits their purposes, they can let you go with no strings attached. So, essentially, you can be fired for any reason or no reason at all. This is why most mass layoffs are legal.

Scary as these examples may sound, the law is generally on the employee's side. In the courts, employees are awarded millions of dollars every year for being:

- Fired in a wrongful termination.

- Wrongly classified as exempt from overtime pay.
- Harassed or unfairly accused of harassment.

You don't have to have a law degree to understand your rights as an employee. Fair Measures, a company specializing in management practices that create fair workplaces for employees, has a terrific Website (*www.fairmeasures.com*) with tons of useful information about disability law, discrimination law, overtime exempt law, privacy law, sexual harassment law, and wrongful termination law.

When you're a victim, it's reasonable to feel angry and cheated. But do your homework before you take action that could get you in over your head. If you think you've been treated unfairly, investigate the issue thoroughly before you make public accusations or hire a pricey attorney to file a suit on your behalf. Once you have the facts and understand your options, you can set out to protect your rights with confidence and conviction.

Fireproofing Your Bridges

A few years ago, I left my job in HR at a food services company because of irreconcilable differences with my manager. On my last day, I went into her office to say goodbye and brought her a little gift. I told her that I was truly sorry things didn't work out and that I wished her the best. Boy, am I glad I went through the trouble to smooth things over, because I later went to work for a consulting firm that was competing for my old company's business! The fact that I had left on good terms made all the difference.

Violet, 29, Michigan

After the stressful process of looking for a new job while you're still employed, accepting an offer is a huge relief. At last, you're free! You probably can't wait to share your good fortune with the world and tell your boss where she can shove that evil assignment she gave you last week. You might think that because you're leaving, you don't have to worry what people think of you anymore. This is not the case. Unless you want to erase everything you've accomplished since your first day on the job, your departure must be as strategic and deliberate as your arrival.

This starts with your resignation. Under no circumstances should you let on that you're leaving before you have a signed agreement and official start date from your new employer. If you jump the gun and blab to everyone, and then your job offer falls through, your best-case scenario is that you've got egg on your face. The worst-case scenario, of course, is that your boss is insulted enough to fire you. Here are some other suggestions for making a smooth exit:

- **Tell your supervisor first.** You want your boss to hear the news from you, not from someone else in your department.
- **Give two weeks notice.** Stay for the entire two weeks, unless the company requests that you leave sooner.
- **Be modest.** Don't alienate your colleagues by bragging or chattering incessantly about your awesome new gig.

- **Don't insult anyone or anything.** Whether it's true or not, show that you regret leaving such wonderful people behind.

- **Stay on top of your responsibilities.** Remember that you're accountable for your work until 5 p.m. on your last day.

- **Continue to adhere to office protocol.** You worked hard for that corporate persona, so leave them with a lasting impression of professionalism.

- **Review the employee handbook.** Understand what you're entitled to in regard to benefits and compensation for unused sick or vacation days.

- **Organize your files.** Make it easy for your colleagues to find materials, so that they can transition your workload seamlessly and won't need to call you at your new job.

- **Do a great job training your replacement.** Your current company has paid your salary for a year or more—you owe it to them to leave your job in good hands.

- **Don't take anything that doesn't belong to you.** This includes office supplies and work product that was not developed by you personally.

Many companies request that departing employees do exit interviews with HR. The person conducting the interview, who probably doesn't know you from a hole in the wall, will usually expect you to divulge why you are leaving and how you feel about your experience with the company. When it comes to exit interviews, the general rule is: If you don't have anything nice to say, lie. Stick to official business as much as possible, and if you must provide constructive criticism, proceed with tact and caution. While it may be tempting to use the meeting to spill your guts about the company's difficult personalities and insufferable policies, don't give in. Once you've made the decision to leave, airing your grievances won't do you a drop of good, and the risk of offending people is too great.

The most important thing to remember when leaving a job is to fireproof your bridges. It's a smaller world than you think, and you never know when you're going to need these people again. And who knows? Maybe you won't even like your new job and will want to come back someday. At the very least, you want to be able to count on one person at the company to serve as a reference for you in the future. During your last few weeks, do everything you can to leave behind a squeaky clean reputation. Be conscientious and thorough as you're wrapping up or transitioning projects. Even if you're leaving because you can't stand your department, act like a team player and keep your negativity to a minimum. If your colleagues take you out for lunch or throw you a going away party, congratulate yourself. It means you've handled your departure in exactly the right way.

Chapter 10 Take Home Points

✓ **Be proactive in dangerous situations.** If you suspect that you are about to become a victim of a layoff, take action before you are officially unemployed. Use job-hunting tactics (such as compiling a power resume and networking for job leads) to get a jump on the situation.

✓ **Avoid job jumping.** Be wary of changing jobs too often. Hold onto each job for at least a year before you consider a change. Individuals who switch more often become known as chronic job jumpers, and employers avoid these candidates like the plague.

✓ **Master the transition between jobs.** While you're in the process of transferring to another position inside or outside the company, be discreet. Don't change your patterns, talk about a potential move, or engage in job-search activities in public. Conduct yourself as if it's business as usual.

✓ **Make a graceful exit.** When leaving a company, the most important thing you can do is fireproof your bridges. It's a smaller world than you think, and you never know when you're going to need these people again. During your last few weeks, do everything you can to leave behind a squeaky clean reputation.

Bibliography

Alexander, Michael. *Networking: A Mentor/Apprentice Guide*. Edmonton, Alberta: Novacom International, 2000.

Benson, C. Sam. "Your Management Success." http://www.coachwithsam.com/success _management_style. htm (accessed February 2004).

BlessingWhite, Inc. "Leading Successfully." Princeton, N.J.: BlessingWhite, Inc., 2000.

Carnegie, Dale. *How to Win Friends and Influence People*. Hauppauge, N.Y.: Dale Carnegie & Associates, Inc., 1936.

Chambers, Harry E. *Getting Promoted: Real Strategies for Advancing Your Career*. New York: Perseus Books, 1999.

Covey, Stephen R. *The 7 Habits of Highly Effective People*. New York: Simon & Schuster, 1989.

Danielson, Diane K., and Rachel Solar-Tuttle. *Table Talk: The Savvy Girl's Alternative to Networking*. Bloomington, Ind.: 1st Books, 2003.

Ellis, Albert. *Feeling Better, Getting Better, Staying Better: Profound Self-Help Therapy For Your Emotions.* Atascadero, Calif.: Impact Publishers, Inc., 2001.

Goldfried, Marvin R., and Gerald C. Davison. *Clinical Behavior Therapy, Expanded Edition.* New York: John Wiley & Sons, Inc., 1994.

Gordon, David. "Suggested Salary Negotiation Guidelines for Recent College Graduates." http://www.collegerecruiter.com/pages/articles/article 257.htm (accessed February 2004).

Hackman, J. Richard. *Leading Teams: Setting the Stage for Great Performances.* Boston: Harvard Business School Press, 2002.

Lavington, Camille. *You've Only Got Three Seconds: How to Make the Right Impression in Your Business and Social Life.* New York: Bantam Doubleday Dell Publishing Group, Inc., 1997.

Robbins, Alexandra, and Abby Wilner. *Quarterlife Crisis: The Unique Challenges of Life in Your Twenties.* New York: Penguin Putnam, Inc., 2001.

Sheehy, Gail. *Pathfinders.* New York: Bantam Doubleday Dell Publishing Group, Inc., 1981.

Weisinger, Hendrie. *Emotional Intelligence at Work.* San Francisco, Calif.: Jossey-Bass, Inc., 1998.

Index

About the Author

Alexandra Levit has spent most of her 20s in Corporate America. She has most recently worked in marketing communications for the global software firm Computer Associates (CA). Prior to CA, Ms. Levit was an account manager at Edelman Public Relations Worldwide, where she developed award-winning PR campaigns for *Fortune* 500 clients, including Microsoft, Pfizer, Philip Morris, Procter & Gamble, and Unilever. Ms. Levit graduated from Northwestern University in 1998, and she resides in Chicago with her husband.